TOKYO BUTTER

ALSO BY THYLIAS MOSS

Poetry
At Redbones
Hosiery Seams on a Bowlegged Woman
Last Chance for the Tarzan Holler
Pyramid of Bone
Rainbow Remnants in Rock Bottom Ghetto Sky
Slave Moth
Small Congregations

Memoir
Tale of a Sky Blue Dress

Children's Books
I Want to Be

In memory of
Mama Flaudee
and for Alison
who gave me reason
to get in the lake
where Deirdre was:
some thanks

(her part in this
is only on the outskirts
of the culture of blame)

Tokyo Butter
A search for forms of Deirdre

Poems

Thylias Moss

A Karen & Michael Braziller Book
PERSEA BOOKS / NEW YORK

Persea Books, Inc.
853 Broadway
New York, NY 10003

Library of Congress Cataloging-in-Publication Data

Moss, Thylias.
Tokyo butter : a search for forms of Deirdre : poems / Thylias Moss.— 1st ed.
p. cm.
"A Karen & Michael Braziller book."
Includes bibliographical references and index.
ISBN 0-89255-319-7 (hardcover : alk. paper)
I. Title.

PS3563.O8856T65 2006
811'.54—dc22

Designed by Rita Lascaro
Printed in the United States of America

First Edition

Search Results

The Culture of the Missing Song   3

The Magnificent Culture of Myopia   8

The Small World Studies Pictures of Cadavers 1839   12

The Culture of Glass   17

The Culture of City Peaches   20

Heads Wrapped in Flowers   23

The Culture of Saving Cindy's Face   25

Postscript Culture of Head Wraps   29

Victim of the Culture of Facelessness   31

Ghee Glee   35

The Subculture of the Wrongfully Accused   39

The Culture of Near Miss   44

Accidental Culture   46

Deirdre in Kinnell's "Saint Francis and the Sow" with the
    Aid of France Bourély's *Micronautics:* Also the Culture of Epistle[1]   48

The Unbuttered Subculture of Cindy Birdsong   51

The Partial Mummy of Head Wrap Extension   54

The Culture of Snowmen   57

The Culture of Mr. Wonderful   63

The Culture of Funnel Cake   68

DEIRDRE: A SEARCH ENGINE   77

A Geologic Survey of Appetite   108

When Jennifer Shows Me a Wave in Form of Question   113

The Culture of Reena and the Bear   115

Mulberry Breath as Proof of the Wave in Form of Question   118

La cultura de pescada: a prediction (instead of promise)   121

REFINED SEARCH (HIGHLY SELECTIVE)   127

Many of us know the joy and excitement not so much of creating the new as of redeeming what has been neglected
—J. B. Jackson

There's more: Nature dissolves all things into Their atoms; things can't die back down to nothing.
—Lucretius (~99 BCE–55 BCE)

TOKYO BUTTER

The Culture of the Missing Song

Cindy Song has been missing since 2001
a new millennium without a trace of butter

—she's now twenty-five, give or take, and likely
employed ethically

based on the sweetness of that face, the pose
chosen from the proof sheet for being sweetest

though she secretly prefers
the one where she looks over her shoulder

with one side of her face framed only by seduction,
the one pose that wouldn't help identify her

in a crowd.

By chance I looked up when her heart-shaped face
was broadcast for less than thirty seconds:

longer looks too risky, as if Cindy were advertising
something, that is not now, just as it wasn't in 2001, for sale,

photo taken when she ranked highly with fellow
graduates, and there was yet no reason
to disappear. She didn't want to be famous

and isn't; after thirty seconds lucky girl is still

in the culture of strangers, occasional handshakes, maybe
she's the one who made my Marriott bed, the sheet fluffed out
a floating landscape, skin of a world

On our first trip to Lake Deirdre, *surely it was snowing   —only swirls*

as gist remembered: onslaught so relentless, I understand blizzards
—4th of July sparkler iced and flaring

blissful in uniformity of light as it descends
without cliffs or treachery onto the mattress

or she may have been in the back room where taxes
are processed and audits are contemplated, away from
indoor palm and citrus trees of the front office
and reception area, their shadows draping ergonomic chairs

into which her hips, like any, could slide more easily than exotic
tomatoes (tomatillos) and nopales into an unbleached linen bag
that cost twenty dollars and will last a lifetime,

the inked brand circle suggesting a bag of rice, flour, raw
coffee beans or peanuts, a bag right out of the cargo hold
of a ship that cuts into waves, slices crusts of water, and also inches
through the Panama canal,

considered a delicate operation, she's just sitting there
waiting for a gentle dentist, everything rotting so slowly
mistakes are made about what is happening:

sliced crusts of water fold like the skin of a chest
she may have opened to massage a heart just replaced
into beating and continuing a life that will end later, ideally
much later, endless gift of persistent coma

that is an iceberg of hope, cryonic tower
different from a burial vault only in retention of warm
visits, but if she's still meaningfully alive,
as those to whom she is indebted in a variety of ways,
some deeply, have reason to assume,
she has been rude in saying nothing, giving no signs
of the fluctuating status of her health and fortune,

so ungrateful

personal comet, hypnotist's wheel, every suggestion cold sunburst

lake acting up, up, uppity —nothing to do with clouds:
its ripples around her toes, my current

that perhaps she of all women could be called bitch
without insult or injury or repercussion
beyond, sorry, likely tragic circumstances:

Cindy cut into by schools of barracuda and other aquatic
scavengers so in need of decay, bits of Cindy floating
like scum, coagulates, a floating feast

of risen remains:

flakes as if she came down from heaven
just as family now contends, Cindy fanatics
and fundamentalists, no hour not devoted
to her absence that becomes, by the hour,
more and more a godlike absence

          a kind of witness and believer protection program

though more certain is that some Cindy particles
fill the mesh of nets as big as coffee or tomato fields
so the nets come out seeming solid even if empty

as if they've been mended.
Pure speculation.

Accordingly, I can see her in the outline, where it's thickest,
of Comet sprinkled generously—like quicklime
where something died and no other consecration happened—
over the stainless steel of twin sinks, completely covering
and filling in a neat rectangle of *Choregirl* brand sponge,
thicker than an actual fully scaled down gravestone

orbits

—*much like salt, spewed   to melt it all: our trips, our Whiskey Island*
mine

that allows mowers to pass unchallenged,
shaving the cemetery, keeping wild blooms to a minimum,
only creeping irises, never any vertical morning glory.

I scrub,
provide evidence of religion.

It could be that she delivered mail somewhere,
went to movies, dreamt of cleaner backs of heads
than she ever saw, researched Mata Hari (*Lethrinus nebulosis*)
and defeated a rumor that she resembled an improved Queen
Victoria, then fed a thousand quarters to slot machines
that were in every state and the few reservations
that she visited between serving subpoenas or evictions,
and attaching liens to paychecks and properties
because her job once was to solve delinquencies,

work taken on out of guilt
over her own protracted truancy

during which she became something other than related to
and obligation, the established way that's done:
running away. Driven away. Taken away
by force, at best of her own will: a superlative

so last act of will and power: Cindy
did her best, a ranking usually valid
for only a year, at which time if all else fails

Cindy at home among the homeless:
story of once being a contender, tale of o-my-
how-she-lingers, maybe a Jane Doe ventilator song: endless
fade

—*some are flawless*
despite how jewels are extracted, processed
flaunted—

of her sweet bone structure:

Cindy Song is a name of a brand of sugar.

::

Next time I'm in Jewell Market, I'll finger boxes
of Jasmine and Basmati rices as a medium would,
last resort at a crime scene

and I really will be weighing something, making
a decision, coming to terms with reality: A hint

of nuttiness, later, in the steam in the kitchen. A love
of almonds. No; a passion. An aardvark tongues

away all steam, restoring a state of blessing
to total erasure.

ice cubes melt
into one full glass

gargle, gurgle

The Magnificent Culture of Myopia

surfaced in trigonometry; it was
the first time I swore
there was no such thing as *parabola*,
no such thing as *abscissa*:

I never saw them.

Chalk in Mr. Ansari's hand
became a magnificent sixth finger, whiter
than anything else about him, whiter than
his profession, his lab coat with *mathematician*
stitched in a roller coaster, an harmonics
of loud letters on his back; even his eyes
(he came close to pass back failure)

were written on, red subscripts
and infinitesimal exponents surrounding
centers dark with explosions of visions
of what could be found only in numbers

He wrote invisibly
on the board, his hand moving along
black expanse like a wave from a baby
ocean and all he did was bless it, caress it,
cast spells against his tests; his name *Ahmed
Said* meaning *God's gift to women* according
to the gestured loops like wedding rings.
Rumor was he never married.

Although he was available
for conferences, I never saw clearly what he wanted,

mouth spray, trickle
down

—snow flurries

8

integers didn't resolve; until I got my glasses
his corrections were too familiar with my face,
exams brushed my mouth as if to blot
excess lip gloss.   From my back row desk

where birds sang me answers through
glass written on with reflection
better than the board was written on, he looked
as unreal as irrational numbers and absurd roots
he introduced

in lessons I thought were about chromosomes
and sexist destiny: everything plotted
on x and y axes
although he insisted nothing was absolute
and constantly shifted values.

Same year at home
I had to get close to a boyfriend
to see faint lines of bar code in his lips
and had to scan his mouth to solve something
meant to be nebulous, the way it was

in church where I couldn't see him
well; he was as shadowy as faith, his edges as unsure
and in that uncertainty, became soft,
blurred, compassionate, betraying the fraying
that betrays good use: a fog in rags
from so much encompassing things
in a somewhat silvery carriage. And now

without my glasses
every night in bed with him, he ceases
to bald; I see no razed patches of scalp, just hazed

get folded in:

more and more obedience
credo:

perimeter, a fuzziness as if he's regrowing hair,
as if he and the room, our whole house of sons, drums,
saxophones, keyboards, replicas of hippos, and canaries
are now beneficiaries of peaches, heirs of fuzz,
scant fur of beginner mold about to bless
bread with blue beards—and we're

about wearing such raiment—we're named
for this just slightly less than magnificent effect
—even rocks put on moss suggesting that anything

can become as soft as memory, distant recollection
growing sweeter with distance, so sweet
I taste (thinking of him and where love that grows leads)
peaches from an Eden just soft enough to be mirage
and every fata morgana.

It so happened that today a lens fell out of my glasses
so one eye strained against clarity, the other refused
to let things merge in blur the way they will have to
if brightness comes with the glare that seems angelic
as it provides light with circular wings; blur and no
distinction, no endings or beginnings, just that escape

from focus, all lines crooked, crinkled, wobbling
as if we're all old with unsteady gait and hands
experiencing *such shaking* when we try to grasp

a peach, *such shaking* as we realize the peach
is more powerful than we are: peach, sweet orb
the drupe of drupes
dangling from a branch on an earth
dangling in a galactic arm playing ball

no matter the raggedness of water during storms
later   on ravages repaired without her help, she just   skated

certain she would not drown

with all the spheres, rotating them
all at once; the peach, is more powerful
than we are—o how we Methuselahs shake
from its magnetism, quake in its gravity,
faint from its taste

when we finally lift it *electrified* to our mouths,
its fuzz much more incredible than the start
of masculine puberty, for suggesting it might
be possible to invent a lamb when that means everything
we aren't, or at least possible to dress
the world as one: softly, softly; even weapons
appear softly, reveal their leniency
to magnificent myopia, softly

the lunatics respond, softly is the therapy
myopically beginning—perhaps it will last,
perhaps visual details softly dispersed
into static will hold, won't be repaired;
a big peach seen from afar is on my screen

when the cable's out   dot matrices peach
when the cable's out   I can appreciate molecules
watching the static   I am grateful for atoms
watching the static   can almost feel the fuzz

under the screen, touch the static, hear it
on the radio once out of clarity's range of belief

in comprehension—humble Blur,
I am indeed an admirer, for it is penitence
I see without my glasses.

solid
landing after lutz, after axel

every time

The Small World Studies Pictures of Cadavers 1839

Almost not there
so much light makes the corner of the world disappear
into the mouth of the open window

      glare, tooth

bottle of chloroform
bottle of mercury

the dead don't mind what happens

      trays

photographic veils, strips of textured light
tear rainbows apart. Through the curtains
leaves turn into reflections of fishes

      gauze

coating of potassium bichromate and gelatin
metal plates, nitric acid

      a vibration in the phosphorous

a cheek still here uncorrupted
only on salt paper

Once there was luminous meat; before

      I make that happen

                every time:

          more and more obedience

pearly slime of silvering bacteria
by the millions and the millions, before
there were such numbers

there were secrets: glowing fungi deeply wooded away
from the pious

who curse the camera
who reform the microscope
with a larkspur petal, a fine
cotton thread

after flesh reveals its treachery:
smooth at proper distance
full of pockets of sin

up close: everyone's a picture of Adam:
that originally singed, inscribed
with a system of forking creases, the pretty pattern
of agenda; so many in the close corrupting look,

    the forks almost seem to move,

        —optical illusion—

travel deep into the psyche,

        —hallucination—

only the legs they are, of crippled vultures

        —hysteria and distortion—
        —bent, the spine, too

                          I clip   unseen wings
                       and there is detritus, snow

               there is no damage

just an hour in the world
slipping away

—the heaven and hell of everything twisted, image
and negative

(—¡so swift the impossible reversal!—)

the parson likewise produces both,
collar of faith black in the death pose
like a neck wound

(so this is the ultimate position
until the power of it holds off putrefaction
no longer)

the coffin his permanent confessional
where he'll have time to try to explain—

as light turns silver salts black
and destroys the clout of assumption
in those first startling negatives:

Fair women are transformed into negresses
—preposterous potential—

and negresses into aspiration
—they gleam under the mark, the stain
has limit, has no depth; *my God*—
degradation's no more permanent than permanent ink

(¡it will happen: great words unwriting themselves!)
(¡great triumphs festering!)
(¡worms feeding on them as on corpses!)

flat on our backs:
        if we really are angels
the weight of wings
                will pin us down   *proof: sometimes*

no more complicated than blasphemy
performing an autopsy on faith—

so sure of the future
devils turn
and see how bright they are

      in negatives

how benevolent they are,
how truly extraordinarily godly
to accept abuse, to hoard persecution
to personify wretchedness
without compensation:

the selfish wages
of doing it to become a savior

The camera catches a lie:
a negress' epiphany, her readiness
for heaven

((and under that, hidden even in x-ray: satisfaction
that delays her going there))

the stomach's so small an ocean
that what is swallowed bobs, a buoy

for each effort to dispose of evidence
even that one is Christian sucking down

      the consecrated salt wafer:

              the same as risk:

              we look across lake and see no end
              so cannot speak

it's true then, this after life on the table:
the angels are just dead negresses

whom light has cut through, the Jesus star
just her in five gleaming slices

a vibration in the phosphorous

as if prayer (that also wiggles
into and out of tight spots) has thrown a lifeline
to the serpent.

It is a shame to cover this face.

ending the spell of not ending,

our voices, our words unable   to seem infinite
not that we require infinity of anything

The Culture of Glass

Thanksgiving 2004: I'm thankful for

Columbo's eye, Peter Falk's indivisible
from the other's vitreous dupe that he can pocket,
rub into, off of, and shine the crystal eyeball after
it subs in a game of table pool. Oh yeah!

The future of fortunes is manufactured revelation
of a snow globe: when the right someone gets his hands
on such a world, that world is shaken to pieces, the glass

is tapped in the aquarium, semitransparent arowanas remain
inexplicable, a tapper's desire breaks out: oh to become glass,
to slide the foot into a transparent baby slipper arowana
and dance with a prince whose glass toenails
shatter when he runs after glass-footed beauties

born that way, skin so thin it hides nothing
without actually being clear, sneak peak
at the friable optic nerve, the components

separated only by glass
through which all seen becomes transparent, criminal
activity obvious, the put-on of opaque alibis
exposing a fear of crime's transparency:

finger prints on the latex interior of the gloves,
imprint of a face on the wrong side of the mask:

at some level, a matter of seeing eye dog versus unseeing
eye dog, culture of breed, hole-in-the-wall expectations, cash
transactions, motel by the half-hour versus extended stay

—we require only that lake be big enough to stretch beyond our limits

(one full glass)
we required obedience

Inside, snow clinging to me   melted quickly, water content

17

opulence just to sleep there for real

with seeing eye dog sleeping on a braided rug half-under
the bed of a blind girl, the girlishness not an issue,
the dog not meant to be her guide into decisions, just
crossings to which she becomes committed independently,

regarding the cool dark of evening, the lapse
of the feel of light as day's form of breathing,
getting illumination off its wide chest
until able to face again the responsibility of light
that even this girl must accept behind glasses:
day is hers too, given by an internal clock
that wants all the bright hours, odor of rising,
flowers opening with the bakeries, stunning
synchronizations, a pas de deux, she steps, dog steps

into the crosswalk at the same time as a man heading
toward them with coffee, led also but by the Arabica, hookah
descent, descant now to the caffeine
that doesn't adhere to the glass mug: it is all for him,
her too if they merge at first sight: the world of coffee,
the culture of glass

bottom boats, success:
liquid assets: if solidity is the basic state

that matters, it's obvious what happens:

The dog retires, seeing what canines see
for himself, fleas cross
his coat without help other than his receiving
no special treatment,
tied in a twenty-foot yard frequented most

less than that of a tear

yet measurable: trace

by sunflowers, each seed
like the eye of an insect.   An alley of a yard

that from time to time becomes a crime scene
in the blink of an eye

                    the glass one melts last.

                    just like permanent transit,
                    that I maintain, looped fraction of second

                    between falling and arriving

The Culture of City Peaches

From my house: Teresa's peach tree sprouted from her roof.
If nothing interferes, this slow start of this world's Angkor Wat
might make it, roots like thighs of every world's biggest woman.

The peaches were ripe when they matched Naveen's face
twelve houses down the odd-numbered side of the street
where the Mabreys had only Coke or root beer
with every meal, because they were Primitive Baptists
and fruit flavors were spiritual pollutants
—as were questions Naveen couldn't ask.

The women Mabreys covered their heads
in the presence of their patriarch; he was the only thin thing
in the house. On my first visit I walked into botched kidnapping,
what seemed a bag was thrown over my head when one of my feet
got past the door. I used shampoo
that smelled of mangos and guavas,
chewed Juicy Fruit gum, smelled like an orchard
because of what age allowed me to spray on: atomized
goodness of Motts. Yet Naveen was proof

of marital corruption, para-dox: beyond belief: a location
her father needed to be possible, yet without consummation
the sanctity of the union could be too easily dissolved
in court; all this contempt stemmed from
the tiny less-than-an-hour bang
in which pleasure displaced prayer, blurred good graces
accounting for the fuzz all over Naveen, a trace of fleece
her father, who respected only holiness, called evidence
of Naveen as the Lamb of God's lost-on-purpose sister
condemned to be a peach head to toe, not just perfect peach

—stay here

but I stood by the lake just long enough to wear a snow crown
then walked home with my father

buttocks, but she covered only her head, hid well in contrition

and might have succeeded   had their dog's persistence
not gnawed her bony toes through the nights. His fleas
were her living necklace. Mosquitoes bit her
in linking rings her father recognized
as a sign of French hootchy-kootchy harlots he'd seen
barely covered with a claim of exotic dancers—*if only angels*
were rare—so he remained at war with the world. If only
Naveen's well-fed beliefs had been hungry
instead of satisfied with explanation of sin spots
for her freckles, suspected transfer from a banana, her mouth full
of potassium that father should know best, as only he
had manhood.

::

My yard's plums were long and thin like tubes
of midnight. The whole yield of the tree could fit
in one small basket from which I sold them
as the world's most unusual pickles,
smooth shaved, without bumps unlike craggy chins
and cheeks of most shaved skin that dark. Miracle
pickles, sweet as something else.   It worked just fine

until the tree of that life in my less-than-a-tenth-of-an-acre
yard was criticized for being so small and producing
such a stingy crop of life slipping away. *Purple meek*

and mild peppers; peppers of conscience and modesty
worked better when I worked the next block.

where warmer, I was still royal, I was also wet

and Deirdre cried
when I called her   —loyal—   just to tell her that—

::

Next door were apples, green ones and blushers
on three trees to which all children were welcome
while waiting for, usually mothers first, to come home
along a trail of cores.

::

As usually predicted because it usually happens
Naveen has withered, become unproductive pit,
kernel and root of every fruit tree being gone
from that street. No more Ball jars of juice
to define that culture, no more making it fresh
legs straddling porch railings and folding chairs,
arms operating paper fans with paintings of obviously blessed
medium brown families of believers from the funeral home
around the corner, in part because these things
are not needed. There are other sources
of Boolean algebra's restriction of variables
to either true or false. Decline had to follow
when unison peaked when everyone drained their jar
and said *ah!* because every *ah* was a star, a pointed peach
of Naveen's unstoppable puberty migrating inside us.
Every inner sun rose, day broke

from every mouth.

flakes lined up in arcs   *(her eyebrows)*
row after row   bleached covenants

Heads Wrapped in Flowers

The Easter hats usually exploited gardens
and even when I took mine off, artificial bluebells
were braided into hair

just as they were (white lie)
when Deirdre's son dropped petals
into his mother's casket: one landed
as useless improvement of her mouth.

Years before, Deirdre and I ducked out of service
went to Little Italy's Murray Hill and slurped
things marinara with our decaf to support her crush
on Hill Street Blues' Ed Marinaro who played Coffey

      who wasn't quite the palest thing in her life
      considering what breathed down our necks
      the most inhospitable air they had

      but we had anticipated bad breath,
      we had assumed a garlicky existence

because miracles we then believed in made vampirism
just as plausible. No flowers on the checked-top table

wilted because of atmosphere. From a distance
the beret we saw on a stranger was telling us
walking wounded

and images from former Persian and Ottoman empires
say the same thing, distance failing to be what it was.

We learned Tigris and Euphrates
to help us learn the flowering of existence.

We learned fertile crescent
and we are somehow still amazed

by the fertility of experience: fully-swaddled
babies shaken like perverse maracas   to silence

instead of make the music of rupture persistent:
light bulbs bandaged then fractured under wraps
and again and again those instruments

for crude concerts that parents applauded
with crackle that amplified the filaments' pitiful fizzle:

We didn't have to go much further to love Batman,
Spiderman, Zorro, the Lone Ranger, all masked men
illicitly patronizing convenience

stores

as I do for the implication that merchandise
has been skewed for the expediency of customers:

heads shrunken

and wrapped in price tags, Styrofoam, satin
and certificates of authenticity. Real

old-school prissy passengers

in long-finned convertibles wore nets on their heads
that when wind-whipped became fully bagged

as nets changed position, flimsy umpires appeared
stricken, the net a prototype of shrink-wrap

on these Sunday drives.

The Culture of Saving Cindy's Face

Cindy Song has been missing since 2001
without a trace of butter, lavished instead

with *talc and vapor, moisture from a bath*
that Cathy Song spied, seeing her as Utamaro's *girl*
powdering her neck, where she is still elusive,

faceless, a universal back of head, hair piled
like fan-back chair reserved for company
that doesn't come, hair twisted in relaxed
whiplash curve

like blackened arroyo (her hair a twist of blackened
wicks). There is an ear that doesn't have to be ear
except the logic of its placement, for the lobe is not typical,
the flattened end of a lever that begins just under the chair,
that if lifted would also raise the chair, perhaps freeing
small birds though, if there, they've been at ease nesting
in the head, enjoying free range of wider shoulders
where wingspan became possible. Stone-faced, equally

at home in gardens that old cemeteries become whether or not left
alone, stone girls on pedestals, cracked wings shedding pebbles,
studding the ground with fossilized eyes. Possible source
of the powder with which she powders her neck, adds
substance; she is delaying decay as avalanche. I am also stalling

so as not to have to deal with the lack of face. If not respect,
it could be shyness, demure approach usually successful
that is at work, but I doubt it, since embarrassment or despair
about facelessness would supercede a classically feminine
approach. There was a need to classify

such births as ordinary for the Andaman Islands
with a falsely documented evolution that parallels genuine
independent evolutions in Madagascar. John Mandeville
had revelations of the gloriously grotesque: a precedent
established by John the Divine on Patmos,
so discrediting Mandeville for not having voyaged literally
doesn't wash, and arguably his small habit of hallucinogens

self-prescribed to fortify his weak constitution
was a vehicle which did transport him. More accepted

is an account of such a no-face birth in the fifteenth century
to a woman from whom such deformity was expected,
she'd been accused of every known sin,
and some secretly admired her (I assume) for creating new ones,
wondering what it might mean if her talent could be diverted
to the good, falling short of calling this diversion salvation.

The child didn't live
long, and the facial plane wasn't flat, but none of the features
fully popped out, as if they were retractable, and had retreated
into little bunkers.

To get at the mouth behind nonexistent lips
required pokes and surgical travels not then perfected; the cry,
some say the baby did cry, and left the midwife dead (the first honest
stab at cry—it really did pierce) was as from a well the baby
had fallen into, the face indeed seemed to have fallen, a typical
first-soufflé face, eyes presumably could look at their own
orbital sockets and see some of the brain
as a cave of mammillated stalactites

though the baby, considered unfortunate and condemned,
born this way to emphasize lack of innocence and humanity
(which the lack of innocence should have confirmed),
the undescended testes no help in proving anything useful
to a case for consecrated burial, had no language,
nor did anyone else, for this condition
that was thought to be devoid of human condition,
given the thin evidence of forked tail insemination:
The skin that buried the face

though thin was more elastic than usual, a stretch
not prone to rupture yet more delicate than nylon stockings,
so it was easy to poke most anything through, a fatal
fingernail of failed midwifery right through that face
sealed in opalescence associated also with angels
though none had been captured for examination, and at
that point, there were not any more advanced alien studies

so the mother, though no one actually called her that,
couldn't claim forced copulation
with voyagers coming to earth to plant their seeds
—and where better than inside so much ego,
when relative fertility is compared? Also, better to resist

comparison that might have had some validity, realized
those too aware that Mary herself had given birth to something
that exceeded humanity, no gospel writers emphasizing
His normality
but rather how divinity manifested itself—even so, He did
resemble Mary, that's who everybody said He looked like.
This faceless child of Germany in truth perhaps better resembled
the facelessness of God who doesn't see with human eyes
or hear with human ears, & so forth, exceeding limits
of human sensing way more than bees, bats, dogs more on
His level of perception. That the exceptional child

did not live long was good, and perhaps arranged:
a smothering
although facial features were already smothered
by skin that already covered it like a sheet pulled
to cover up the dead with a less offensive muslin
easier on the narrow range of human sight.
It may have breathed, this strange boy whose name
was withheld for fear of cursing any other Hans.
Strange Boy
seemed name enough. But to call Utamaro's girl a victim

of facelessness isn't quite right; it seems she'd need just to turn
to show her face, except that it's detached, lays on the mirror
the faceless girl holds at an angle that could not catch
her own reflection, so the mirror's face comes from elsewhere
and the faceless girl looks beyond it:
the mirror is aimed over her shoulder,
the face in it is there as something on a platter, as a cameo
for a giant, whitened lily on a reflective pool without current,
without need for anchors, not far enough out
to have to look for harbor that should not be the default position,
and what's on the platter looks like Cindy Song, exactly

the way that I remember Cindy Song, missing since 2001,
as Utamaro divined she would be when he painted her face
and only her face in the eighteenth century, finding
what a girl would lose in the nineteen-eighties when born faceless
to a more resourceful family, the luck of existing

when there's more skill in exploiting resources, in taking
advantage of both medical and mystical advances,
so her parents lifted the face
from the painted girl who offered it to anyone in the future
who might know how to make a face stick, take vein and root
in the rich soil and dirt of evolved flesh, and become real:

Utamaro's girl did have a mask
that Cathy Song found irresistible, its extension
into a *curve of shoulder like the slope of a hill*
set deep in snow
in a country of huge white solemn birds.

At the end of 2003 I saw that face again detached:
a photo of Cindy that was all face, as if lifted again
from the reflective platter thousands of atoms away
from a neck being powdered into existence,
and I'm not going to find Cindy with that face

that she has taken off, that flower whose wilt
she has discarded, unable to put it back on
after stepping out of her bath so refreshed,
like somebody else, the molt behind her reaching
the drain.

Postscript Culture of Head Wraps

Her knuckles exasperated, my aunt as dead as Deirdre
cried for a washboard: it had been too long
since the last scrub's knuckle-peel

through which she gauged conversion: responses
to the fear of bleach to which she'd become immune

so did not whiten, did not use it to fake vitiligo, did not surpass
her rest home cook's uniform like her sister Maid's and sister LPN's

all beaten by Black Muslim women on Superior Avenue
where we were too, without the centerpiece

that makes a difference, especially since it sits atop
Black Muslim female heads like a linen pyramid or
sphinx. The riddle of faith in stitches.

Her knuckles exasperated, my hand squeezed
into its own exasperation, we walked through

all that Muslim whitewater on Superior, through all that white-
capped spun flax sea of hospitality and urgency of nurses

everywhere, superior treatment of that location, though
whiteheads are also pimple eruption when sebaceous glands

are blocked—I've always been stuck with dualities,
wasn't pulled into the sea that could have claimed, that must
have parted as women aren't navigable
unless they move or are moved, and I was no force, still

am not ready to wrestle with *Soft as Silk* and *Swan's Down*
cake flour, boxes of contenders ten years in the cupboard

waiting for promised attempt at scratch, probably full of pontoons,
webs of temporary ropes in the ring, towel thrown over the head

to let dough rest, just to be let near sanctuary, to blend in
with immaculate covering of civil unrest in facilities of praise,

white head wraps kicking back

any light hitting them, these white heads also frosted
bay windows, conspicuous on the street, a recess

inside where the personal sits; if allowed
to happen, the cake can still be cake, the rise

not necessarily compromised if webbed flour
turns out layers of lace, a more patterned cake,

structure less that of foam, more that of washboard
also present in magnification of linen's tight white weave.

Victim of the Culture of Facelessness

To call Utamaro's girl a victim
of facelessness isn't quite right

because of what depleted uranium is doing
to babies in what used to be Babylon; it isn't quite right
to call some of the variations faces

because the markers aren't there, the noses,
the eyes, the mouths—what face without them?
what irony—though it isn't quite enough

to call it ironic—that when faces may be uncovered,
cauls and veils slowly lifted, there is nothing
underneath some of them but blankness

as if cauls and veils had been erasers. To call it
clean slate and fresh start isn't quite right.
That there is voicelessness goes without saying,
will have to go without saying

though other parts of the body can produce sound,
especially offensive noises as if to express dissatisfaction,
normality, disgust. Legal documents can still

be signed as blindly as ever, attorneys will still have power
and will still be below the threshold for determining
what is absolute. International frogs

are sympathizers, the odd-numbered legs,
even-numbered heads; the frogs quietly take on
entanglement, linked to consequences

of what is done to infants no matter how well isolated
these events are to certain cities and beliefs. Particles
leak. Every day, more

codes to break, to access codes intact under them,
Paul Tessier a good example, his smashing of cadaver skulls
against stone walls, some blocks already stained enough
with grapes and white peaches

though those peche blanc stains were invisible,
but he sensed them, so smashed
skulls there, in locations accustomed to upheaval
on many scales, blind moths flew into them

and made a splash of wing like paint
—not every night, but often enough—
and Tessier broke the code by breaking skulls
to learn the pattern of cranial and facial breakage,
the preferences of fracture,

and then the motivation to learn how to reset bones, tiny pieces
as delicate as picking the delectable from escargot
whose shells Tessier could crush in his hand, and did,
to overcome his patience, his idea
about skull fracture entangled with how he ate snails,
how his vocal cords expanded in a culture of red wine
just as mind should expand; entanglement can deform
and reform but doesn't have to. And yet

twin Muscovites reportedly born this millennium
have been affected, one born with no face, the other
born with two, reputable physicians
would have the world believe, and the obvious,
which has been a part of none of this,
so can mix with nothing, is not a consideration;

the extra face can be removed and transferred, but there
is hesitation in the name of preservation
of once-in-a-millennium occurrence not mistaken
for second coming despite the timing. The faces are layered,
the same blood vessels route through both, loop dependency:
they are his nourished personality, they already help
him dig deeper:
                        the deeper face faces inward,
though the stack, not being aligned perfectly,
allows one eye to see behind him peripherally.
He is making money already, a medical first,
still called medical impossibility, a moral first
for the genuine literality of two-facedness.

A fee to see him, study him, figure out
how to burp him, to see for yourself if he vomits

from both mouths. A fee that helps his brother
whose life is easier, pampered, because there is nothing
to see, to pick out his face from the crowd,
it is necessary to look at the doubled brother.

It is hard to say which products might be right for him
to endorse, which sales might double
because I have sympathy. He can not give up any of this
to the twin born without complexity,
eating through a tube just as insects do
sucking up nectar
that could all come from the flowers in the room;
his toes twitch as if he smells them. Face parts
or whole face collected from the generous dead

can somehow be attached or combined
with conventional prosthetics; he has an optic
nerve, olfactory and auditory canals, set
of drums, plumbing, the underground
rigging, the pipes, shallow roots of milk teeth, two
shallow holes (as if vampires assisted) doing
the nose's job so that he breathes, airway is there,
everything that should be below the surface is. Growing

up by Chernobyl, his mom loved the passage
of geese. In general loved examples of flight.
She looked for this.
Hundreds of birds could come together to make solid
night sky, separating after many hours to allow light
by reducing and minimizing wings. As if just for her,
perhaps the only one watching. Nuclear waste
flew one day into her soup, and that was that, fallopian
and ovarian hocus pocus and harem scarem, that old
black magic putting on another show. Too many nuked cooks
spoil her broth, so many molecules, billions and billions
of atoms serving her air and everything: try to tip them all.

Even if this is a hoax, it serves some need someone has
to test believability, and to test balance. There is some need
to fabricate it and accept whatever comes because no one knows
the limits of what can come, because in everything is some
necessity: that is the cruelty of jokes and of imagination.

The boys were cheek to cheek in utero, there was a bond;
they couldn't overcome it, when they had to separate
to be born individually, one face came off, sticking
to his brother, stamps do that, that brother keeping
his brother's face, entangled, desperate love

—like divers sharing a tank of oxygen, I want to think,
because that is beautiful, their heads together,
their unity of four kicking legs, their joint bubbles
like fertilized eggs surrounding an octopus
becoming a small cathedral.

Ghee Glee

Each churn sculpts butter differently, marks it
not exactly as a gun barrel marks its projectile
but churning and firing the revolver have more in common
than that which doesn't mark or isn't marked.
I am relieved to know that effort encrypts

that goat's milk soap soothes, goat cheese and butter
combat genetic sensitivities, and like any other combat

offer mixed results

that vary more widely after the freshness date, the best-if-
bought-by stamp. Nostalgia is not exempt, becomes more
and more decadent as time advances: good old turbulent
familiar decades

are historical for children who have nuclear tests also,
ground wars over seas just as rough. Books seem benign
no matter what seethes
behind words the mind can attach emotion to: ink
just bleeds, and pages supposedly inflammatory,
sometimes banned, feel so smooth; more and more
of them are acid-free:

Butter. Pure butter. No need to limit what is only said
thought   dreamed: partial realities that melt like butter.
I feel so fortunate to be part putty: amoeboid butter
engulfing what I encounter, complex destiny because of complex
identity: I am never completely out of place
(many choices for where to shelve this book, each a best choice)

and my presence which must be dealt with gets churned into
the meaning of what occurs there.
Assumptions butter the mind   or coat it so that
what it doesn't want can't easily get through: butter barrier
greased pig thinking   but once on your skin
butter can feel like your own secretion, your own rich oil:
bounty ooze   crown melt —if only there was only toast

in the picture, deli buns, biscuits, croissants, beignets
more obvious reasons to lay it on thickly, but sticks of butter
come architect-ready to build a house, plantation columns
and nothing is easier to sculpt
than pale butter skin all the way through, bone-free, dull knives
glide renewed,   resuscitated: ghee glee. Even some tigers
take on the purity of butter
when sunbeams melt on them   like a web, snare of light

solar churn

toasty equatorial residents

but I don't take croissants with butter other than
what batter subsumes,   internalizes
deprivation also appeals, demands of heritage
(I don't deny all of them
or any of them in expected ways) hardtack homage, pilot bread, ship
biscuit, going to and from difficult places, some in, some out of my league
especially if visited
at the time of day that all shadows are gaunt, as if at least

one parent
is a butter knife: the father

is the usual suspect, related assumptions implicated him
in Cindy's disappearance in 2001 without a trace of butter,
maybe this very butter, withering from the sides of the container

slick with

what was lost to surface. For maximum fun with butter,
that part of legacy (my father an unsalted butter-color man):

a fresh tub for each impression. One for chin, one for hand, another
for foot, each bite mark. No problem: there was always
another butter. Exceptional mortar butter, plaster of butter

every year

Easter butter lamb to butcher gently with polite knives
the shape of oars, shape of skinny hooded priest profiles.

You stuck your hands in, the butter softened cuticles, repaired
dishpan hands, soothed scrapes, minor burns —Mama ran butter-fisted
when I fell off the bike—   was elbow grease

if you wiped it there, and let rings come off as if it was before:

softness back

and some of your innocence

in family tradition of Blue Bonnet, Mazola, Land o' Lakes'
Indian maiden coming at me sometimes in a canoe taken as rescue

craft I was too big for; I could open my mouth, and she, Princess
Whatchamacallher could float right in, down

my throat that with tonsils and tongue offered a take
on southwestern land formations. We used Big Chief
baking powder and sugar, had Minnehaha Water delivered

in jugs big enough to have held fleets of sunken toy ships,
and sold what we called bog water (taken from vases
and saucers under potted plants, spruced up
with Listerine) to those who wanted adult drinks prematurely;

—¡O Deirdre!—

bog water of premature wine not done fermenting had to be
priced by proximity to process completion. After any of this
we freshened the air with Indian Blessing Spray #41

that stank a little bit
and also smelled a little bit like cherries. By not   .

partaking of any butter, not indulging, not giving in
my toast was sandpaper, the usual slice of fossil-sponge
Martian terrain close-up. But it could crumble, could
become dust in my fingertips, could look as if I crumbled
with it, tobacco like, filler for my father's Pall Malls
that he smoked to death, and as if I were butter
—had that responsibility   time to time   I opened cigarettes
scraped the paper clean   and wrote haiku riddles that I rolled up
tightly, my words burning from his lips   easily

gone gone gone

All four slices of my wooden bread
are sanded smooth grain. *Old English*
protected —that oil like supremely clarified butter.
What fine head and foot boards for beautiful small beds

no one fits, only if the size of cigarettes, pack of white-robed sisters
from Virginia   what fine understated tombstones.
This bread may be waxed. O shine. I know who Shine was.
Its lines are durable labyrinths   *our father*

fingers and tongue may follow in cursive spell-out.
That wax, that sheen of get-away

from the path shines my fingerprints
where I grip the bread as loose pages, loose leaves
of suspicious adaptation. Loops under the arches
are a green onion bulb
cross section, innermost loop

like the eye of an embroidery needle
or like sperm-head
or like the hook
that scrapes out early pregnancy

depending on who's looking. The loop made
when tying the ribbons of a blue bonnet

under the chin.

The Subculture of the Wrongfully Accused

Ultimately improved by it: slant light
hitting his prison obliquely

near the state bird's pointed head   accentuated
crest, the black-ringed bill

from which *wheat-wheat-wheat-*   *wheat*
from which *whoit cheer, whoit cheer;*   *cheer-*
cheer-cheer

inspired Ronald Cotton to listen
as in his head, the solitary cardinal   indulged in snails

which seemed like polished fossils
of trophy hog tails   (after prize   butchery)

that Ronald was able to recall,
his hair a mess of replicas of them

as industrious as the state
whose success was poultry & eggs   tobacco & soybeans

as well as convictions:

None as tightly knit as Jennifer's   (not even the state flag)
that she could identify Cotton

that cotton's taking on appearances   other than burst white
of a dense localized haze from which to weave memory, following
pink-petaled start, rather a satellite   dish of a flower, pollen/sensor-
studded antenna protruding from   the center

undeniably; the jury couldn't acquit   Cotton
of its role in documenting and altering   Jennifer's history,

many lives changed

as result of consequences, sensors   that boast duality
of receptor and transmitter: witness: insects give and take, taint
what is put out, taken in; mix

it up so that interrelatedness spreads
and the understandable error of metaphor
becomes less erroneous over time:
eleven years in prison, innocence locked up, protected

although in prison, it resembled something else.
If Cotton strained, he could see the top

of a Ferris wheel on the horizon just a possible
segment of a rainbow the length of a chain

of cardinal feathers

even though it wasn't that at all. The eye witnesses all the time,
even the unseeing eye is turned toward a focus
on black, saturation dense as conviction; the eye

processes, pulls in whole vista to a retinal speck
of convergence

which is to say there is some Cotton in Poole,
some connection, independent shared participation in cold
beer, occasional cards turkey-spread
in the right hand without knowing the other
sank into the seat at the cinema the same way

and sampled Funnel cake at the state fair
within a week of each other

and more than that in common: both being men
and convicted for what men really can and really do, do.

Including sometimes confessions and apologies; cash reparations

after the innocence is free to extend its parameters
to unlocked doors, be an oversized over-zealous white bird
floating down the aisle, its cottony haze lifted
in order to kiss and marry Ronald's calm delight in being able
to take his time

leave his longshoreman's mark on ships
that take some of him to any port in the world: durable goods

such as the DNA whose precision   detects human exactitude,
and could build as many Ronalds as   time would permit

something Jennifer now desperately   wants to do, restoring
what was lost because it was like   something else,

because the fact of similarity   is compelling, convincing;
if connections could not be made,   there'd be no havens, no fugitive
status lost to fusion, no links   to God, no human

murmurings whose   constant echoes
are also the gentle silvery hum   of fans praying
over computer motors to cool them   and also mimic
motion of small wings amplified   to make sound

in the distance much like   the electric razor
preparing a head on death row   clean as a light bulb.

Ronald was prepared to be believed;
he saw the quiet manner of his long days in court
as evidence of his rationality and   contemplativeness

such as befits clergy; a potential   propensity for order,
mercy, the steadiness required to   dispense blessings
mostly on the undeserving without   emotion or judgment
selfishness or preference

while he was being judged guilty for   lack of emotion,
for Jennifer's incontrovertible emotional insistence
on Cotton's being the one—she had   to finger him
to be comfortable within her survival.   No way to mistake
to ever forget details documented in   memory,
the event relived to the point that it   resculpted her brain
into a Cottony bust (he was there   to be the perfect model)

whose reality floated away   in a Poole,
as only the reflection of Cotton

identified as source. A situation   also called (must-have) moonlight.

Here's the new & improved Cotton: eleven years in the making; enough
time served to anger to ruin it; at that   same room's temperature
it became doubt of clemency, pardon: peculiar butter that erupted
as gratefulness for the miracle of absolute exoneration
when his impossibility as rapist   was proven.

Even Cotton conceded that   the composite sketch
bore a just resemblance to Cotton,   displayed a metaphor for men
like Cotton, the seeds of capability   in the structure of the face,
the human repertoire that includes   Cotton
who softly consents to meet Jennifer when she asks him to
funnel her regret and apologies deep into himself, accepting that
she meant no malice toward him   but toward
the perpetrator whom many men   resemble, all
brothers, family

of man resemblance; Cotton's   own daughter, Cotton's own wife
could be in a similar position; no   offense
taken, captivated by the beauty of   Jennifer; her superior logic

refusing to let the crime against her
silence her; as sure, as certain, as   dazzling
about speaking up about mistaking   Cotton for Poole
as she was in identifying   in the lineup
the closest thing there to Poole   the best
available, the incredible   likeness
that memory seized, filling gaps in   the recollected Poole
with Cotton's particulars.   She felt better in her cotton-touched skin.

Metaphor is a form of forgiveness; a short rope of it knots-up
those that can't come together any other way into being defined
by the other. Strange

and estranged pairings give rise to mutable truth
that can yield to both dawn and twilight
demands that things be seen differently.

                              .

Jennifer in moonlight instead of being illuminated moon whose face
was also in Emmett Till's way, but this generation of Jennifer has another side
home late after a day of good faith   in which she and Cotton team up
at a church to speak up about doubt as less a shadow than certainty.

Memory is as accurate as metaphor, an overlay
that always fits something, that like the purest
most sparkling water is too naïve   not to submit
to any vessel into which it's poured.   Just to be guzzled.

Perhaps the vessel in which cotton   becomes a pool
in which North Carolina is shaped   like an embryo:

Humanity still on the brink   of infancy.

The Culture of Near Miss

Because all energy went into making him breathe
dawn was not noticeable

though on the beach it was bigger than anywhere
else, awakened stars stowing away in sand,

low-tide sparkle of a cosmos the sea will take away,
subtraction is basic, the boy's body when movement

is subtracted becomes less, there is hardly any boy
left, his color drains invisibly; it leaves him

to arrive nowhere, his chest becomes a sunken basket
for white peaches (out of season)

through what he's lost, not what he's gained.

::

I loved Jerdy
and if my name's not here,
he won't know it was ever true
love, not that he hasn't been loved
by others

also not present, subtracted from the picture,
and even if he has been loved by others
perhaps he won't be again

unless someone falls for a picture;
that has been done (someone I know fell
for a picture of Cindy Song).

Loving Jerdy now is to love him
in the way that makes most museums mean more
to me, he's not to be touched, ideally

he's to be observed in silence, perhaps
photographed, probably without flash,
and if he's not stolen,

insulting the injury of his having been stolen from,
he can be returned to, sometimes only his outline

while he's on loan and his permanent space
has a chance to discolor.

He travels much more this way.
This way, it's not necessary for Jerdy to breathe.

He hangs.   The museum is closed

on Friday   open on Sundays.

His arms rest   on nails.

He seems as wide   as his length.

Crowds gather.   *On the beach*

his breath fell out of him like stars

When he's on loan   a pale cross is left behind

and he couldn't even see or touch the sky.

Accidental Culture

The blizzard an hour to the west just as promised,
there was time to go out and return before whiteout

with the Qur'an in my hands, the Arabic
beside English also notations of movements of an unborn child,
arabesques of smoke and breezes bathing walls, attempts
at peacocks, botanical bones

that answer subtraction of color, petal, seed,
perfume; recovered whispers of lost roots, shorthand
of ten thousand lunar phases. Right here: necessary distillation
of gather, pluck, knit, fold, unfold, *open, open, open.*

Initially behind the driver's seat, the book
slid all the way under as lane change
gave the vehicle access to a runway
and inspired launch of Flying Toyota, takeoff
delayed with a hit on guardrail: *truck bliss*
knocked down to three whirls
that were all its own pleasure; I felt none
of the spin, saw none of my life
before my eyes, caught a glimpse of a Bronco,
so I stayed with the skid, the wheel to maximum right

with the Qur'an under steady, hard-knock cushion;
my glasses flew—how else?—into the passenger seat
when the airbag punched my mouth, and my right foot
slid from gas to brake so smoothly, black ice
must have been on the pedals too. From the airbags

(both deployed) came noxious incense, brunette smoke;
a truck soon in flames seemed certain, the CD still playing
—*honest to God*—without a skip *Blessed Are the Meek* on track repeat;
to get to where I was, the song had played twice, *inherit the earth*
on impact. It was just science—everything has some—

airbags are meant to pouf with bad air. Before I knew that,
I got out to save again the life that seatbelt and airbag
had just saved, leaned just a little to look into the ditch
with no obvious access but a fall

onto varied weed heights and rock
formations; under snow: a triad collaboration
that held a skyline of uncomfortable city. I sat

with a dozen translations for two hours
before choosing poetry and precious paradox
for twenty dollars:
He is Allah, the Creator, the Evolver, the Bestower
of forms (or colors). To Him belong
the most beautiful names: whatever
is in the heavens and on earth...[2]
As my truck was towed, shed snow
seemed the hatching of ephemerals

like groundsel and shadflies
in the twin worlds of side-view mirrors,
the panorama of distance:
          its magnitude: width on one side
and close, personal shaved vision
on the other. Had the Qur'an not been with me

when [or because it was] truck became an anthracite
misguided missile, the 4x4 pirouette may have dispatched
a leap into the ditch that would have seemed to rise
to meet it, good host to probable demise. Or the event I love

to talk about now and use to divert reputation
may not have happened. I was not

in control of the vehicle; the state trooper
said so; he did not say what was, had no interest
in actual powers. However, he could not deny the silver

indent in the guardrail is a curve where
the left headlamp nuzzled. The other side
is mammary: a metallic udder.

Deirdre in Kinnell's "Saint Francis and the Sow" with the Aid of France Bourély's *Micronautics:* Also the Culture of Epistle[3]

To Whom It May Concern: *The bud*
stands for Deirdre, droops for her too, strange Bourély bowl
within beams of electron bowl, stamens of strawberry tree flower
Eschering well as flurry of nipples; also: healed locations
of fowl decapitations beg for suckling, *even for those things*
that don't flower to anchor there

where *everything flowers, from within,* establishing
the beginning of Nazca, the start of intervention, longitude
and latitude interacting with interest in the other
bulging in magnetic shapes here and there: at top
and bottom in buds of light stretched out in ragged
splashes, glimpses of someone dragged through,
lynched through, vigilanted through
rockiness exaggerated by weeks without rain
or any other amelioration, bud dried out to thorn,
the flower inactive and more remote though present, idea
behind the locked form, armored flower with keyhole
as *respiratory cell of a rose stamen*

on top of necessity *to reteach a thing its loveliness*
beyond what most are willing to see: the effort
of Deirdre to open to a belief in the cantaloupes
available in *wild cowslip pollen,* a picture also
of the aspiration of juggernaut when that is allowed
to flower into Krishna, flower of Vishnu who preserves,
among other things, the bud and Deirdre, who's improperly

embalmed, still, that is, a form of wreck, so cold
in the casket with a pearly finish
easy on eyes, my *hand on* her *brow* in the last half minute
of closure of the casket, withdrawn involuntarily
by those who understood this business from the *retelling*
in words and touch that she is hard evidence that
it is lovely to be a rock of dehydrated bud, seed of disintegration
of a mountain, and that nodule of existence further explored
to access units unimaginable because they are outside

of what is graspable by human senses, the invisible units
of greatest commonality, present in anything that exists
yet elusive to human detection unless details are blown up
out of proportion: *Paris put into a rosebud*
and looked at through an electron microscope in which
names of streets and titles on bookshelves can be read
with ease
                     —Deirdre and I knew in seventh grade
only of the most basic and similar ease in making our Easter suits,
unformed sleeves so much bigger—like ideas—than the jacket's space
for them, had to be eased into it, gently gathered, mild
crumpling smoothed out while stitching over feed dog
& under presser foot without a pleat or pucker:
the sleeves underwent a form of reduction
without being cut down, retaining integrity actually expanded
to perfect fit,—*oh yes indeed!* just *as Saint Francis*
put his hand on the creased forehead
of the sow, and told her in words and in touch
blessings of earth on the sow, all blessings
of earth contained, each a bud in factorial bud!
All blessings of earth in Deirdre, *her thick length* measurable
in the church where no one looked at the ceiling, all flowers too
turned toward her, more baby's breath than when she married
already pregnant, a mass of stems of many buds that explain
what Deirdre's hands will be after many years
underground, *the spiritual curl* and spin on things
taking over *the long, perfect loveliness* of corpses, unfolding

in them, Deirdre too, a perfect accordion, just like
the expanding flowers of existence whose vibrations
of opening produce undiscovered music that requires
inhuman sensitivity to register as sound, the most
profound noticing requires inhuman sensitivity, passage
over thresholds that don't exist for humans
who break so many barriers, even in so many ways,
the Great Barrier Reef still budding, propagating
where it can, recovery showing a particular talent

like the talent of invertebrates that reproduce asexually,
a constricted parental outgrowth breaks off and lives
to have that mature separation happen to it —this happens
in yeasts, helps them promote fermentation, helps those
in Deidre fulfill themselves; for their acts in baking,

yeasts are prophets, they say the universe is expanding,
they say that Deirdre is astounding, bursting
with microbial worlds in a bread box.

The Unbuttered Subculture of Cindy Birdsong

Of course, there are obvious, frankly, reasons that the missing
Cindy Song (since 2001) brings Cindy Birdsong to mind, another

disappearance from my life, though even when she was active
—overly generous—in my entertained days, she was replacement

for a missing Supreme after Diana and then Florence
departed, and after there was some flap really important

to those flapping but hardly worth resurrecting
seeing as she can still sing like an unspecified backup bird,

so no surprise that she's just an afterthought
here because of Cindy Song who can't be here
though CB sometimes took the lead in pop tunes

nobody talks about much unless necessary in trivial games
where stakes can be lucrative, millionaires made

for knowing Cindy Birdsong was a Supreme, as little
as that, though at the very least she was also a daughter

and was probably at least once somebody's lover
and perhaps the recipient of fan mail and hate mail

because she was a Supreme, after being a Bluebelle
at just about the time that there were still Queens for a Day,

though rarely African Queens on that game show, all the royalty
proud recipients of new Frigidaires, Amanas, Bissells, & Hoovers.

Cindy's certainly not the only afterthought; the linen bag
of tomatillos not far from here is another, the shape appealing
in the challenged corner of my eye, contorted as if everything's
taken in the gut; in one version it has a drawstring

that can be pulled noose-tight
then gets turned upside down
into ideal bag over

shrunken head about to be hung
though shrunken heads don't need redundant trip
to the gallows

especially since they usually travel better, to non-publicized
auctions as they make their way into collections. The Jivaro
of Ecuador made them best, *tsantas*, skull-less heads
rather like hairy dates and dried plums, a kind of rum cake
with lips stitched, a kind of sturdy yarn cup. The majority

of shrunken heads I've seen have shar-pei faces
or something that's found in the dark

center when a radiation-altered sunflower head opens,

though this majority needs to be qualified,
as I've seen only a half dozen shrunken heads

outside of movies
and most of those were monkey heads (mostly in Toronto)
though they weren't saying only monkey, resemblances
& so forth, though covering up and burial aren't necessarily
more respectable than trophies

unless the corpse proves incorruptible and becomes patron
saint of compact embalming—not that, though it could be,
the goodness of John the Baptist is shrinkable. Mostly

thinking must be revised: like many, I once thought everything
on television was in television, shrunken to fit into the box

in which case Cindy Birdsong would have been the most
remarkable of the shrunken heads, singing up a storm

the way she did the last time I saw her
& loved her in color that could be changed,
at volumes that could be changed

but she could not be enlarged
without getting out of the box

of static and cathode rays, streaming
electrons, without giving up

hordes of atomic
and subatomic groupies.

The Partial Mummy of Head Wrap Extension

gets in the Crimean War, with the bandages
on the little princess's father's amnesiac head

as tonic against damage underneath,
sterile tonic against infection:

       Florence Nightingale's system
       of circulating antisepsis.

I see that wrapped dome
and then I can see the Capital

and the political in all landscapes,
snow wrapping the head of the Himalayas
while flowers thousands of feet below
blossom into feet

that seem to be bathing in gardens; insects
swarm the equivalent of rain

after I see the wrapped amnesiac dome,
plaster cast of a fruit bowl
as if the sick man tries on breakfast.

       Fathers sometimes falter.

       Some fathers say they want to falter,
       they are wrapped up

       in y-chromosomes threatened
       with extinction. Their policy.

       Deirdre is not upset, she's put her mark,
       an X on her son to compensate for her loss
       of husband, his Y both excuse and reason;
       Y-not?

The male defining chromosome was previously thought of
as a wasteland where genes go to die. [4]
> There is a needed, Deirdre will also tell you, *quest*
> *to bring respectability to the Y* [5]

The Y naturally seeks itself, wraps itself in itself
as if, Y's logic, to cut back on mutation.

What chromosomes do, does not sound respectable:
no men are moral at the molecular level.

—Perhaps some wear the weight of that on their heads.

Pairs of chromosomes swap genes to complicate things
for mutation, to foil some elementary paternity,

but the Y is stag, and swaps with itself,
self-same sequencing, just reversed as in a mirror,

up and down the double helix streets, a do-wop group
on every corner, looking good, sometimes veering off-key

and mutating themselves out of a sperm dance
to go with the *please Baby, please Deirdre* song.

Because it has to, why else? *every man's Y contains*
600 DNA letters that differ from his father's,

and there are fifty million letters in Y's finished sequence.
Y mutates, perseveres, and becomes infertile

thousands of times more than the normal mutation rate,
almost making it possible to understand why Deirdre's
mutant Jerome was so unfaithful and insolvent. He had 600
additional ways to twist the alphabet of his promises

yet he failed seventh grade math, Miss Barufaldi's class, the grading
on a curve.

He wrapped Deirdre in regret. He brought her battle
in bed,   didn't butter her up
and she didn't bring it up   except to explain
choices she didn't forget she had

until she died, and as far as I can tell, then promptly

forgot everything even that

The Blue Men of the Sahara are often also
better men
picking up tint from what they wear, what
they are seen in: their revelatory traffic
of behavior

in which so much is risked, so they wrap
their orifices against evil and dust storms
and the relocation efforts of grit

and vault their thoughts in turbans.

It must be easier,

under the *obmubilatio capitis*, under the imposition
of the veil

under the turbans and wraps
of luxurious moral and chromatic color

to let a peony span the mind, to become
a flower at home in a garden of exoneration:

a little bliss-head   with a pistil and a stigma.

The Culture of Snowmen

Obviously, they are frozen manna men

except that they don't come to earth
that way: famine relief

out of the sky like boxes of pure grain shot to pieces.

There are many metaphors useful
when avoiding confrontations with what blown up men are like

since avoiding blown up men is not allowed
by men, a rule of asserting possibility, in the range
of what becomes necessary.

So there is the totem of men of snow,
a sacred short life respected by great winds
like the Williwaw that can separate snow
men into billions of cold factors, lift each one
so that each cell flies like an insect, swarm-shroud
of white locusts ascending into the crop of clouds
either succeeding up there
or falling dead-white back to earth.

It's just that the Williwaw can pick those snow men apart

and seem to give them what men usually mean by grace,
the men who must be disassembled by insects and bacteria
or burned in order to rise from the factory of body.

Snowmen experience no reentry tussle
as did historic astronauts

whose reentry vessels were more like killer meteors
than like snowflakes that seem to favor matter transfer:

reduction to atoms reassembled into banks
and into men after arrival,

though of the available men
astronauts are the men snowmen most resemble,

though they're much more like Styrofoam insects:
three spheres: head, abdomen, thorax
also made by men mostly in their youth
wavering around the prime of life

science of making duplicates, substitutes, gods

of ourselves, Frosty the Snowman alive
then melting like any other immortal aspiration.

Vexation is much more solid, those stick arms
that are stakes crisscrossing the heart

of snow

only; had there been any other variety of heart, the arms
would have impaled it.

The melt of them, the puddles
that say *like you real men we too are mostly water*

though how little that uplifts and comforts

when men have watched their jealousies come
alive, the substance of snowmen each a particular

separate parachute   at first
falling, then gathering into a billion-fold collection
that has common purpose, function:

scarecrows caught in personal avalanches
enlarging avalanches where

The fall of flesh has meant burnings, crimes
and sanctioned punishments.

The fall has not improved the men that fell
even though they arose

for it is nothing to get up from knees
to conclude contrition

to become human

and enter the caves, start fires, the industry
of making men

from animal experiments, the generosity
of pigs, even the pancreas
also of Chinese hamsters to which men are indebted[6]
as men evidently are supposed to be
since most are in debt, sinking

except that since we sink in space,
the hell below is above earthly orientation too:

the squall of snow proceeds from that.

Snow drifts down
of geese, crazed ones devising ways to pluck with fervor

and madness, molt blizzards and hazards

yet for all the frenzy, nothing binds
the down that warms, handfuls

don't become molt-balls
and don't melt with the snowmen they may have decorated:
the down as fill, as patch when winter
misbehaves, runamuck temperature way up
when winter should remain authentic
down time:

temperature, snow, prices of revealing
swim suits falling, light falling back, dark's portion
larger, chopped wood going up in flame, distant
snowman with marshmallows on his arm-sticks,
blackening edges like paper early in its burn,
and it's all hickory air, the scent thick
in everything, almost a third dimension: new skin

as if to replace what burns away.

As if to supply the flavor of being involved.

Snow also fills gaps, ground extends whitely
to the windows, pitched roof covered with uneven blank pages
glistens while I wait for snow to fall solid, without space
between, interlocked plates, gear flakes

before the landing resolves into mishmash
that is shoveled, pushed, plowed, skied.

There are certain bears, certain snow leopards, cranes,
certain albinos and mutant colorless things
(clear as bells)
that could get lost in the substantial bellies
of gluttonous avalanches of snowmen

were it not for the evidence of hooves, eyes, tongues:

the rules of digestion, the rules of awareness,
the rules of entry and exit, rules of cohabitation,
rules of forensic investigation

that work because nothing is silent, everything has markers,
tracers, echoes as vestiges of vespers,   existence is territorial

by nature

snowmen tend not to budge
once they become men:

They remain men until the melt
down or seemingly more cruel and deliberate demolition.

Though men are being made, no qualifications
are required of the makers,
and there are no requirements for the product
for which there is no quality control

except the motives of the maker
whose like or dislike of snow cones
could be either detriment or advantage
for either the maker or the snowman:

the making of anything includes the making of dilemma.

Is the universe parallel, curved, distorted
like a perfect arrow that doesn't exist beyond theory
trying to nip everything

so that truth can't ever meet folly, each traveling
uninterrupted in opposite directions, each claiming

to move from past to future, one flat, one inflating
and sagging like a saddle? Is it any of these?

The birth of snowmen is nearly always at home.
The death of snowmen is nearly always at home.

They usually don't live long enough to have birthday
parties. In places of permanent ice, men aren't made
with the gusto and necessity of makers who must handle
more radical temperature fluctuations

though men everywhere make angels often
called other things until metaphor makes angel possible
and anything else possible,

and there is really no other way
that anything can be possible,
especially astonishing reversals.

When they threw snowballs at me
before they were the men they would be,

assured by the throwing;

when in their gloved hands
snow became rounded cooperation,

in sun seemed polished
as the palmed asteroid-ettes arced toward me
full of trajectory,

I was in the middle of the making of universe
yet could not grab

planets, comets, whizzing by, a snowball
becoming spiral galaxy when it flattened

when it encountered my face, and adjusted
to the curvature of that space

that genius had to understand, before anyone else could,

the theoretical being,
the snowmen out cold

warming up to an idea.

The Culture of Mr. Wonderful[7]

First there's innocence as professed
by his profession: selling boatloads of flowers

that out of his hands become adornment, snacks,
overtures that profit this dealer of vegetable matter,

some petals displayed around the flower head
like a hand of cards: the gamble in anything.

Then one must look more closely at that hand
the flower's been dealt as it becomes what

Mr. Wonderful's been dealt: the family
business, not lucrative all the time; he's not

in it for the money, but for the pure pleasure,
since there's often nothing else, of ferrying flowers.

> *Many tulips close up on him at twilight as if they hold small*
> *empty*
> *eggs: elegant voids—or maybe some inner peace that*
> *probably*
> *would be rounded, but not a ticket or passport to anything*
> *outside the garden; pollen drops from what sky there is*
> *inside*
> *onto impersonation of a velvet floor*
> *and would be at home in an hourglass: the whole*
> *night spent as gist of what I thought came out*
> *of successful tonsillectomy.*

At water's edge: a battalion of white peacocks,
the feathers the most elegant spines

blown back like umbrellas blown back
and contorted like supposedly double-jointed girls
in a circus desperate to be spectacular

but also like, as if the double-jointed were not enough,
partial jellyfish; that is: jellyfish that result
from lobotomy, the ragged half brain of tentacular nerves

or more decorative radar dish
to spy on celestial activity out of the ordinary,

to eavesdrop just as the plane trees just beyond
the startling white peacocks, even their eyes,

are doing: bare branches in the blown-back position
of the peacocks' feathery array

with which the plane trees collaborate, each
translating the other and transmitting mutual praise.

Mr. Wonderful is a captain completely unaware that I know of him.
His expansion that he knows of is a little Mr. Wonderful

whose resemblance extends to a smaller boat
on the other side of the lake.

Some of his petals, the ones most like daggers,
excusing the softness, are dipped in poison

because some poisons make the most beautiful ink
and is necessary to write the name of his lover

on the active surface of this lake, the water under his boat
moving like her under him, so many underlings move him,

yellows, oranges, pinks, lavenders spilled here like congealed
volatile oil, wacky pie chart gone fractal

perhaps just to be popular
and on the up and up still rising, garnished with blush

of pollen that is dirty and nutmeg-colored from a rubbing
on Mr. Wonderful's fingertips before dispersal

and the impression that rubbed pollen
could be a grating of his skin for no reason at all,

and that could be why he'd do it.

The trick is to get his fingertips there; after that, there's no trick
to what's visible under the microscope: fortified spiked
walls
of a labyrinth, the innermost curl somewhat a spirochete,
and saying that, it's clear just what to picture: artistry transfer
to brushes with syphilis, lues, late treatments, penicillin
success after gross disfigurement, many diseases
seem to establish blossoms on skin, leprous flowers
tended in special, colonial gardens. Pet vectors.
There are spikes and hooks
in the fortress of Mr. Wonderful's fingerprints, torture
labyrinths,
caches of poisoned intentions unless this is taken another
way:
beautiful loop of embroidery, the head of a seahorse from
afar,
silk fins present though unseen.

Under the microscope some flowers have bones, there's
druse
inside the cells, crystalline inclusions made of the stuff
of kidney stones, and in the flower cells
skeletal druse looks like starburst: an angular and pointed
sub-flower that gathers light.

There remains the simplicity of his selling flowers
not yet milked, still full of perfumes.

They live in marigolds. They live in cyclamen.
When customers sniff, they pray into the petals.

Some flowers are poisonous without this wonderful help:
Barbados nut, the seed of a hairy botanical thing,
at least 55% hell oil
and a taste that can be craved, almost sweet,
though belladonna, though the berries of lirio
so much more purple than plums—nearly black,
about to burst with coarse sugar—look sweeter
and are a source of Wonderful's ink
as are the ruddied orange sometimes berries of assumed
pure lily of the valley linked to devotion with bell flowers
each of which seems a chapel

where a corpse might lay drenched in flowers
all because the lily was thought to be wild garlic
and was souped for what turned out to be a last supper
of that soup and a salad of anesthetizing monkshood

leaves and radish-mimic roots so that the Dundee cake flavored
with the same to finish off the person finishing the meal
was not needed.   Nothing was left   to chance.

Fish are not stupid, that is not why they're hooked
on Wonderful's supply of flowers floating with him,

slapped occasionally with water Mr. Wonderful scoops up
until sequences of float, scoop, slap, dip, rub, disperse

blab and blurt out ritual, and the wonderful boat becomes
a church on waters of exile

where fish die with Wonderful's poison in them, white bellies
like sails no better off than the up-bellies, quite unsail-like sails

for being waterlogged inadequate islands
ideal for water bugs that don't need such refuse

to be refuge. Dead fish form plump alphabet:
a spell of *Rima* on the water.

Her name drifts with the bulk of fish belly
mounds like variations of mushrooms, stems submerged:

stubby legs: small white tables, even in such shrinking
Rima becomes part of everything

because there is such a thing as her signature
on everything, poisoned in a way   of looking at love

that went nowhere, did nothing, was only what
Mr. Wonderful was in: a little box like the one

that contains diamond solitaires, sometimes hidden
inside a flower to bypass ordinary circumstance,

not quite successful because it still involves dirty work:
the demolition of flowers to get the boat full of seeds:

so wonderful,
so much greatly magnified dust.

The situation can't be cleaned without ruining everything:
the thicker the dust, the more depth to wonderful living.

The Culture of Funnel Cake

Trapped—in lumina
what is available at the center of a sphere:

clarity of zygote

—only those born too soon crave a translucent curtain:
$$milk\ wash$$
[—creamed blank eyes, vichyssoise up to the neck—]

There's a cuckoo clock in the crystal ball-room
above the rocker where a mother fills snow globes with her
$$milk\ wash$$

and split coconuts full of paint chips that look like feathers
fall leaden to cover transparency
although that is much better than nakedness.

::

First thing that morning of corrupt eggs:
the overwhelming brightness of ellipses

and the unfulfilled intention of bald heads
that hatch sweat

positioned as would be precious unguents
formulated in vivo, animal embryos and placentas,

venoms & vectors in that our sweetness has been compromised
by the ability to think of alternatives

to salvation and healing
which can be avoided entirely

as it was first thing that morning of corrupt eggs
when all I could think about was the overwhelming brightness
of bald heads. Ostrich eggs on necks. There was a rumor that

S__ could lift her scalp since she was born with excess skin, so shortly
after birth, her seamstress mother established a pocket, and into it
literally stuffed what she wanted her daughter to remember:

notes
preceding those headaches
for which her mother gave her
notes

on which her mother wrote: *this is a pill, Girl*
and *this is another*

elliptical offering: women of eggs and coffee cake
and olives, the coffee in the cups as level as anything
could ever hope to be:

the way spiders navigate the web
every line is a tightrope, one line also a drawstring

and when it's pulled, the web draws up into a net
that holds an invisible ellipse
that remains stiff after the egg is cracked,
after the light bulb is shattered and the living daylights
inescapably become homemade maracas

shaking at the carnival, shaking up
the funnel cakes like swollen tea-dunked webs

inflating cosmically:

::

To live is to embrace danger of rapture:
In the search for something impossible, for something
that could not possibly be stunning or compelling
there was finally just dozens of corrupt eggs

from which life as I knew it could not come out,
as under the shells, which turned out to be valence,
crackpot models of atoms,

there were light bulbs
in which tungsten (saving the day from barrenness, personal
extinction) somehow could breed and inherit and mutate:

      chicken leg filaments   beak of current
      circuit body   light-blood   corpuscular photons

So to turn on and off the light, to compel darkness
to behave like tides and gigolos   was to experiment on the living:

$$\left[\begin{array}{cc} \text{in vivo assay} & \text{in vivo assay} \\ \textit{taglio vivo} & \textit{taglio vivo} \end{array} \right]$$

::

—Consider that what arrives next millennium or two is the cut that is alive,
that thinks for itself that it wants to do this: slice, divide, multiply, each piece
somehow alive, quick-clone, swiped from routine how-cells-do-it

—except that a woman's extracted eggs are not viable after deep-freeze
at the peak of a woman's blossom—she should be no more
than thirty, the ideal woman in 2005 —but maybe the 2020 version
will be different, surely because of what 20:20 has to mean—

—though radiant in her is idea of egg revival, thaw
during her autumn:

          the menopause rising of funnel cake, plump endometrium
          squishy support of implantation of embryos with skinny funnels
          of pipettes

most women who wait don't become biological mothers, not
at this time, their eggs corrupted by age, elliptical clock-face sagging,
                            old tulip
dolled up youthfully, a respectable lie
that does not affect the eggs
still bald, unfertilized, empty as a crystal ball
saga of impossible daughters. Unfertilized eggs don't freeze well,
can't thaw as well, not yet. Tick tock.

—I have noticed that blisters seem to contain milk
and Leeches will gladly suckle:

This is the culture of compensation.
The culture of because we are not yet immortal.   Pray.

::

Now then:

ex vivo   *ex vivo*   *ex vivo*   *ex vivo*
          from the living   from the living   from the living

an edge   a rise   a ridge   a chasm ▬▬ a surrogate

solution. As youthful as can be ✚ An elliptical spark
to a spermatic comet comment:
Halley's comes back virile after thousands of years
spreading seeds until death

cosmic pollen: jackpot
cosmic yeast: jackpot

The way it is: the roll of his dice, his balls.
His juice. A man's timeless worldview.

::

Understand: embryos must be frozen, stockpiled, not eggs
that won't survive: sparks not intentions, actual ignitions
have the present chances.

Fireworks at the fair say fertility is this brilliant exploding
garden of light. This electric wow. Shocking proposition.
There is incessant winking, flirting, amps of botanical evolution: bright
future: Imagine: light-bulb shaped plant bulbs bursting incandescently
into spring, tungsten stamens, electric roots

on tulip bulbs that screw into and out of sockets
dark as dirt.   See the Ferris wheels

as fulfillment of plant-hoped version
of space station: cartwheels of color, petals drop like burnt out
photons:

overloaded lacewing wings unloading powdered sugar
when they crumble over the plate of funnel cake

the color of thin syrup, a tangle of dead leaves, or notched pig ears
left after slaughter   like flowers for the dead,
three-lobed pink clover

     —within this, the [sub]culture of eggs,
     there's the winter of government intervention,
     powdered eggs, servings of overload, flub grid, outsourced
brownout, New York to Canada, surplus lacewing wings scrambled, yellow heaps and
heaps
     like mass suicides of chicks

       —here a chick, there a chick, everywhere a chick-chick

except in the wombs of women who waited.

::

Meanwhile: indulgence: amuse ourselves, all thumbs
make miniature moose tracks picking up bits of funnel cake
between annihilations of fake moles

in whack-a-mole to win a piece of humane taxidermy: stuffed
animals, only harmless plush

made of fossil byproduct
hanging just as butchered parts hang

for inspection
that may or may not be carried out, 50-50 chance
only in how you see it

—be advised: the [sub]culture of E. coli might be closer
than it appears in those mirrors with which carnivals are navigated, in-
fertility taking elliptical tickets, all of them.

::

—The initial cut into the ground to remove fossils, dinosaur eggs,
time capsules   can be triangular as if digging out a church
turned upside down
in the bright world in which pollen spills out wattage:

the stems are live wires, hanging around
the white cage of turkeys with tails spread into kites,
each feather as charming as lady fingers
mangled into funnel cake, pecked at, nibbled, as if being polite
to something, as if being superficially tolerant is not also being rude
to something more important.

—What will it be, motherhood while the body's made for it, an ark
for it   or take on board two gametes neither of which is one of your kind?

—The next generation won't suffer this
                    (something else, but not this exactly)

::

—You can't sleep at night because   Every hue and nuance of sunset
is represented in the carnival of botanical flare-up. Visual wallop.

Electrified vertical gardens of mesh
is the nicest way to explain electrified fences while

looking ahead to a time of electric flowers,
pompoms of lightning, radiant cabbages   spilling searchlights,

looking ahead to massive transformation, upheaval,
the world without us, freed from our genius

that is capable of wrecking, restoring, and inventing
simple truth

of us which is root: panorama in dirt
something to which to attach something else
that has a chance.

—At some point in the future: new schemes of reproduction, new
forms of life not subject to emphasis on the fallen state of dominant
living things.

The advantage to the pyrotechnic population approach: fireworks don't fall,
they fizzle. The bright-biggest seems lassoed lightning pulled

into flowers of controlled glow, chromatic gunpowder
to make night-hot exploding roses, luminous mum-heads
flare flagrantly, round as roulette wheels

as aspects of the lobed brain—*o the mass of it, density*, just white and gray
            matter

                medulla oblongata way down low

and so musical as it's been named; the sound alone
seduces, grabs—say *medulla*, say *oblongata* while eating funnel
cake—*o euphoria*

knowing at the same time how the funnel cake grabs grease
and good eggs to become a smashed papery-looking flower on a plate
garnishing resemblance and remembrance with demands
that everything be as flower—*o open wide, o orbit of blossom, o electron pulse*:

                —in the seduction of likeness,

    I called things that shouldn't have been called at all
    —radioactive flowers; I sure did; just a regular atomic girl, born
    into atomic fuss

over fireworks (sure; they were really big ones, but something
                managed to give birth to them

                    —what did Nagasaki look like from space?
                from there: could you take the whole thing in?)

that have evolved (to live with it & other choices made)
into essence   —of dahlia

  (which is dusty yellow)
  (which is cheek over-blush pink, sick
  flamingo pallor, red & white Niles-wines
  coming together, associating)

              —of cyclamen
(which is red or a cluster of magenta echoes)

—each light bulb a closed mouth sealed
  into the culture of pout

      —stuck in a pout

that pushes up like a flower   in the expanding universe,
    the carnival of acceleration, the Canaveral of opportunity

into space usually occupied by nose: ripple of punched in the mouth
swollen like a hothouse variety of something. (radiant funnel cake look-alike)

         From a distance it's a too-bright field
       so I keep looking knowing I'll adjust to the intensity

normalizing it : a simple garden
that, quite garden-like, seduces with blue, green, golden
bulbous heads

of women in burqas : lights in the darkness : the loss of power : grid
flub : removable flames : fire distilled

    —after losing most of its properties
      except the rich color

that delights those chromatically challenged, limited
to the spectrum, supremacy of Mr. Biv (the owner), his
rainbow of burqas stretched out to dry

while he sleeps with the under world: lingerie easily peeled
until all that's left is the magnificat in the form of beautiful flowers

      (so hard to tell apart in their sweet cover, canopy
      of fragrance, canopy of color, the culture of bouquet)

beautiful, beautiful flowers that he gave her, anniversary
of his ability to give them.

::

      I try to sleep well no matter what, eat well, so it's
      culture of fresh herbs in the culture of acceptance:
      I chop them *in vivo*   *in vivo*   *in vivo*:

      heads from skinny necks
      and peppercorns are crushed black light. It helps.

      In the center of the funnel cake is a dark inverted steeple.
      Black-light house.

—When the funnel cake's been eaten down to square,
the whole remainder is picked up; on the way to mouth
is held over eyes, its fried mesh, fried grid like edible burqa look-out,
its fried mesh, fried grid breaking up the monotony of seeing
a single scene, its fried mesh, fried grid putting together a puzzle
in the culture of funnel cakes: metaphor
is king of advocating forced symmetry: ropes, chains
full of burqa look-out opportunities:

there is no isolation, no exile, no uniqueness
it can't cure, finding not dreaded duplicates

but equivalences, *almosts*, and *not quites*, *make dos*: in the name of surrogacy
the Tree of Evolution spikes and branches,
veers; therefore such amazing twigs: those angels, those demons,
those despots and lovers among us. Those Bakers and Smiths and Dryers.
Imposters. Understudies. Fabulous Fakes. Those (delicious) funnel cakes.

Deidre: A Search Engine

She went to Italy

and then she died

a woman with her,
that none of the living-
without-her
knew, had bangs:

overwhelming sight
of bathers, & sail   why not?   limp fevered petals
                                    left was only caves   gathered into barrettes
                                                                   like hair
viewed at the impossible angle
of things without noticeable end   hers
also no finale   was dark water
                                    mud flaps of the big rigs   stiffened, sealess,

                                                                   fishless; just hair,
                                    for cover   fine, flexible protein
                                                                   strings
not unknown to clouds
the side of it a thin line,
a cut
                                    her ex-husband's laundry   paltry with shreds
that from distance   where he left it   and rags of atmosphere
is horizon and necessary   folded like cliffs
to purpose   leg holes of his briefs   virga over Patmos
                                    like craters
she laid figs on her lips   whose lost substance   like something smug
                                    and credibility
                                    became moons   without reason

in the Presence of Mourners.

Every toadstool was uprooted.
Neighbor children's fingers were so fat

each would grow into a pig.
There was that much faith—wasn't it that?
in moonlight

that filled buckets during one session of pleading with it
to give and yield and fill

Deirdre—

What is it for, this reflection? Delight?
Everything can't be for that?

Twist, shimmy, worm into it, force

a delighted huddle

a fence of crooked spines, guardian nurses
as the children, retarded, sniffling, rubbing bottoms
of their noses, a finger of pig
curved like an extension of upper lip
poked out like a roof over shingles of teeth
white as nothing, those teeth pure exception

pulled up the toadstools

that looked so much like nails
and needed so much to be hammered
into something, but up against those teeth of pure exception?

Later that day: open house, the realtor
showing it to strangers:
                                        Deirdre's house
yet there were no strangers to compromise loss, everyone's in
a related stage of grief or recovery, choosing to look at it that way,
unable to look at it without a way to perceive

moonlight   (7 April)

in fog sweeping over the bay
where seven were killed in a planned boating accident,
motors cutting flesh in the way of a machine's priorities,
skin like colonies of plankton and baby seastars, baby jellies
and seahorses as transparent as innocence can be conceived,

on the surface, where the skin was used to being
part of the water's shimmer
that Deirdre's fingers disrupted
to make circles as tight as the curl of her hair
in the Italian humidity that everyone else raved about

huddled around ruins.

                                        (Gloria's lilies)

                Deirdre lived beyond that lawn
                as green as any lawn had ever been,

                when green became necessary
                in order to bear

                the conviction coming clear   (his own testimony)
                in her husband, whose charm had been a scam fortune
                earned in espionage, sanctioned marauding until
                his orders came through as an astronaut, only till then.
                                        (faithful Deirdre, at the

mailbox
                                        everyday, country-style,
                                        on a stick by the dirt road,
wild
                                        lilies wilder there than
                                        on any other part of the
property,
                                        vining up the stick, into the
box,
                                        postcards with pistils and
petals,

                                        no return address, on Easter
Sunday   more anonymous flowers)

                                                                    79

And then Easy Street, really in her town, a cul-de-sac
where families rode bicycles and ate sandwiches in & below
anonymous trees,
and meant to have more of those moments, and tried not to
blame
each other for successes or failures, for the obvious reason
of misinterpretation, the quietest moments occurring
between men and women married, but not to each other
though it did prove that seeds didn't really care where
they were planted, a flower would be flower wherever
it grew Buttercup, Daisy, Crazy Phlox and Peony,
deadly
ricin in the castor plant that has a habit of flowering,
Nerium
oleander, rosebay, wolfsbane wild and cultivated,

it's settled:

his orbit was to be her engagement and wedding
rings, but she'd have to do the actual traveling in
neglected circles.

His baby was how she found equator

of her ample middle
her plum of forgiveness

that moved during the wedding as if her unborn son
was in love, the enticing vow wowing him, *cleave* and *cherish*

whose syllables were part of babytalk.
Mother and son stayed close

when bombs fell

on schedule everywhere that they were falling

the little bombs, vials, ampules
cracking open in gas chambers and in veins, traveling
in her estranged husband's truly blue ones (but no truth serum).
color of guilt, rainbow of guilt

as her water broke
     along with old records.

     He was the only man she knew not impressed by rivers.

Was it a cool drip into his arm? Can there be dependence
on sodium pentothal? Did he feel that shrunken submarine?
every torpedo of what he considered relief? Did he imagine impact
of one more dream coming as true as truth could be to someone
who didn't socialize on that level of bluntness

where things got fat and ugly (especially a good third trimester)

just as decaying mirages did, wide oases, broad
palm leaves misplaced being at the tops of trees
where they suggested mature women's hips
despite where they were

just as there was always weather

in which it was safe to fly a kite: go ahead,
nothing's there but electricity, the secret of light,

he urged, her birthday forgotten, be a kid again, paid a kid
five dollars for his kite struggling in Woodhill Park, gave her magic

of a silk scarf from around his neck (office gift to him, secret
Santa) (the only one from which he pulled, eked
out everything else he gave her) to be the kite's tail, the secret
of maintaining flight. He was not exempt
from horizon, was himself the vanishing point:
some kind of kooky convergence
of implications of everything
with evidence of nothing, source
of redemption for a few definitions.

Deirdre's man was a good man   (or she wouldn't have become
involved; she called him *Sweet Jerome* for a reason); it was good of him

to get it off the ground: kite, coffin, virginity;
a full carat crystal of quartz in which so much is blurred
when slipped on a finger to complete
a second, third, fourth proposal

each followed by ceremony. Bought the largest ring he could
so it circles the finger and needs adjustment—*uh-oh!* see
his wad of bills for what the jeweler loses, *sorry, Baby*; *blessed insurance*
—the heck with getting another just-a-symbol; Deirdre already felt like
a one and only;   the only one to endure this:

                the diamond cutter
                and fire eater
                lived out their natural lives together
                Her fingernails were overtly
        porous.
                Molecular gaps
                for some reason
that didn't matter to science
                so science left it alone. Left to their own
        devices
                each nail was a slice of bread, full of
physics of foam,   (despite emancipation)
                really soaked up olive oil and balsamic
concoctions   especially
                since that was what they were most
frequently in:

                Because bread was part of her, there were
severe implications   for her bones: French bread arms,
challah thighs   and she didn't want
                to lose that the way she'd already lost
                a dozen angels
(baby cakes) (little Debbies) (Ho-Ho's) (Anita Baker CDs)
                and custard cups, as if those were related
                losses, the quantifiable
                and the unquantifiable right next to it:
     do-it-yourself clones.   Boxed set.
                Dragonflies picked the fire eater's
                nose, the singing made the secretions
        buttery in the mind
                of the fire eater, and that was therefore
        the scent given off,
                something the dragonflies in this vista
        adapted to.
                A dynamic system. Everything pitched in.
        Pinched. The waist cincher really pleased him.
                Crimped. A hallelujah every now

and then, but it was called many things,
the effect didn't change, on and on.

She sucked the oil out of her fingernails
and bit them,
oil-softened sucked toast, old wheat.

He didn't complain, for his palms had evidence
of old irrigation systems that had sponsored wheat.

Sometimes they rented a catamaran

from a jewel thief and smuggler

because they had to take care of each other

and they could forgive the occasional brawls,
fistfights, because those came with

the compensation

of flowers that grew as tangled as anything else
when left alone to decide what growth was: where,

how, why

blossoming is such a good thing, a fist opening, closing

pumps the blood

circulates fragrance: look out now! insects & their
inspiring public quickies,
botanical promiscuity: her husband bee a man

—Do you understand why Deirdre threw them down,
why she plucked the arches over her eyes free of

skinny petals

careful to uproot the follicular seed? She wasn't about to grow
any trifling clones of thorns

but everything blossomed, opened, swelled

to the point of exposure, revelation; she didn't see it coming,
but it got there: a way to get in, gnaw, peck, excavate, unfurl magnificently;
think: *onion, onion*, skin coming off in layer upon layer of radiation sickness,
long-finger white radish prosthetic ingenuity blossoming in desperation
to make the music of this meaningful by transcending its plain truth: radishes

wet-noodle tied to knuckles, and these radish out the scales and chords,
the garden sings and there is rapture

and Deirdre is a bride

and is buried in something even whiter:

the uniform of Eastern Star mysticism
that meant nothing to her before she died
because she went to Italy
when it wasn't safe:

no reliable beliefs in her pocket   of nail crumbs.

Everything about her dead says Order of Eastern Star,
and by order, everything is tightlipped, silent, under
the rigmarole, autopsy because she was supposed to recover.

Biggest flower of life was an aneurysm in her brain
still collegiate when she's turning fifty
whether or not she's ready, treating herself to Italy, a villa as if
that's what it's all about: hills that won't be shy there, one shoulder cozy &
familiar with another, tessellating on every possible plane and the space
between them, tessellated time, no gaps, but maybe not the fill of choice, free
will and chaos all chucking out symmetry, overriding and entangling
     similarity
in which to plug undesirable and desirable details, inspiring and
     uninspiring
specificity: which is which? If it touches Deirdre, it's relevant.
Building blocks.

The fourth funeral of her life

Too many flowers for the cemetery, the mortuary, even for the realtor
who had told her to leave some fresh flowers in the rooms, but this was overkill:
carpet, upholstery, wall paper sprouting, china and bed linens sprouting, facial and
bathroom tissue embossed and sprouting, sunflower showerhead pulsing out seeds,
petals melting in the heat, tropical, and weary: not this much disease could come
into the world at one time and be called
a *blossoming* instead of *epidemic*.
The next day

arrived just as promised, shaky awakenings among the family but valid
despite insistence that going on without Deirdre was impossible, patterns of pink

light writing her name

                        on a   sky check

vanishing, the usual slippage

                (we say she's up there, but we go to the cemetery)

                as the clear raw egg becomes opaque and tasty,
                a threat to sanity, too: I really don't want pretty grief

—without her being there, nothing is the way she would have wanted it,
a whole world not to her liking, whole and complete without her

whole and complete without butter
no one thought to buy,   a circle of damselflies circling an invisible column

                only air there

for damselflies to necklace   (she's up there) (the melting light)

                        on a morning without other butter
                        to spread thicker than their patterned wings

much like a drawing of a chamber of the human heart without color or definition
other than arteries and veins, goings and comings

that when illuminated bring forth a possible heritage of lightning:
ineluctable paternity

and craving of guava jelly of a translucence that says *gimme some*
bootlegged jellied moon moth wings
so is trusted for that, saying what nothing else says, so is genuine for that

when it's really at this point

        extreme butter deprivation   *(only the melting light)*

and is curable

        so I prepare to go get some, straying from the mourning:

the future
dipped in a butter bath is appealing

as it melts, I think I'm making mascara
and reimagine everyone worth reimagining with two big butter-pat lips.

        Kiss the bride.

Butter Nile I see
and many lesser butter rivers
churned up by paddles that otherwise
would have claimed canoeing.

        Pyroclastic flows contain heart-of-the-earth butter
        that overtakes towns too close to that; windows

        before breaking
        hold the image of butter like molds.

    House of butter glass.

Sal de Onodondo built a model of every church in Nîmes
out of goat butter from a caprine line
descended from those goats at the nativity
chewing on the hay that at birth foretold of spiky halos, capra.

[at various times, *goat* has translated as *ghost*, *ghost* as *goat*
            and continued after the error was exposed
            for the sake of the poetry,
            for the beauty of leaks,
        for the conquest possible only through translation]:

(There is a language with only one word, so everything
becomes that. Dear, Deirdre: I am learning to speak it.)

Lesson 12:   The Ghost of Butter

                    is with me on the Google Odyssey

to get to the bottom of Deirdre, starting with a link, in her last email,
to Guinea, an offer wanting my approval for her to delve
in Improved Shea Butter Processing and Technology Training
of farmers in Dabola. One volunteer.[8]

Then a click to Burkina Faso of shea butter as independence
which may not also be salvation; Butter is not eternal, a stage
of milkfat, it can be acted on

                    according to this protocol
                    or that protocol

For Sale:

549-   Vane, Hydraulic Lift for butter boats.
14563-   Vane, Mobile Butter Boats, aluminum, for use with butter churns.
20633-   Votator Pilot Plant Margarine System, A & C Units.
16634-   Westfalia, Butter Churn Model BUC 3000, continuous, 7,500 pounds per hour.[9]

Wonderful butter boats move through solar reflection, section it
into wavering hemispheres; bubbles from life even lower
pop into the separations like modified solar flares. (Softly
phosphorescing phytoplankton hordes like dollars melting
in butter glow-rub.) (I wouldn't know this if she hadn't died)

In the Basic recipe for Herb Butter [10] that I bring to family gatherings, mostly
funerals which become reunions

> 1 teaspoon lemon juice or a few gratings of lemon zest
> is   optional).

Whatever components are decided on, the way to progress
is the same: Chop, pulverize, cream, blend; Shape as desired and
              chill or freeze.

Here are five of the Suggested combinations, one for each point
of Eastern star:

> * Tarragon or fennel, lemon zest, and parsley for fish, chicken, or eggs.
> * Savory, marjoram, and parsley for beans, veal, beef, corn.
> * Rosemary, savory, thyme, oregano, marjoram, lavender, and garlic
>   for grilled meats.
> * Calendula petals, chives, and parsley for chicken, rice, or eggs.
> * Scented geranium, rose, or pinks for toast, scones, waffles.

Each point points to variations that converge:
the makeshift mortar does the trick, things do adhere, follow form,
we grew saline crystals on loops of string—how's that for rosary?
I remember peanut butter taking on science project honoring ingenuity
of Egyptians, Aztecs, George Washington Carver, Deirdre
taking second place at Robert Fulton elementary

> then her project doubles as a winter bird-feeder.

Peanut butter is a tributary of the Butter Nile fanning out,
sticking the political universe that might be stuck
in a growth accelerator annexed to time expansion:
things hatch, blossom, become too big for britches of origin.
Once stripped of them, they can't be put back on. Her *Skippy* Sahara
is to scale and more stable; next time: some reality
for Valhalla.

Pinwheels of accordions are recommended for the increase
in every direction, taste folding into taste, fiddleheads sliding on butter,
cooked livers folded into grape leaves, like packages of opossum embryos,
compact baby pygmy bats, dozens

on heirloom spoons

for a picture printed on glossy photo-sensitive paper
as if enhanced with butter sheen

—Deirdre's face too, on the obituary, a yolk in the folds
of Eastern Star-white yardage enough to make a dozen sails, one
enormous flag, if wrapped around and around her, would have made
a mummy, web-sticky cocoon from which insects really do emerge
underground, Deirdre the hostess, but too much like plaster meringue,
and the paralyzed whiteness seemed ready
to spill: the intention was foam. Hope resists exact fulfillment
which would be its death. Some set crests of yardage seemed goats
trying to lift their heads, Deirdre dead
with remnants of magic all over her, failing, white folds bulging
caprine; her fingers turned under holding small crosses
were the beginnings of ram's horns

where before any of that, there were peanut butter sandwiches
like huts in her mouth while she sat glued watching the drama
of South Africa fold and unfold, mimicking a heart, acknowledging
that everything has untold history, there's no way to tell most of it
but peanut butter is texture of what's true:

>   Most rural [South African] women grow their own nuts and grind
>   the peanut butter in the traditional way, using a guyo;
>   a large, flat and smooth stone used as the base
>   with a smaller round smooth stone used to grind roasted nuts.
>
>   Quality and standards have been improved through introduction of
>   plastic jars (previously the women were using old glue
>   [and] paint containers and other used plastic containers).
>
>   To improve productivity, a number of manual and electric
>   peanut butter machines (for producers with access
>   to electricity) have been introduced. [11]

This is where I met the Babcock method
and let it take me where it could, further than

>   determining the percentage of butterfat or milk fat [12]
>   in the Guernsey stream; her own
>   was much more blue

and as it was for Rima Babcock whose line led to Deidre,
and who ate peanut butter sandwiches every day
in the Depression, fortunately liked it homemade, chunky,
some peanut shell here and there
so that Rima believed bird bones
crunched between her teeth

so that Rima believed feathers
—thick ones that bore most of the responsibility
for the success of flight—
stuck to the top of her mouth   which became sky

and she swallowed birds   guiltlessly

until her teeth hatched and her mouth became nest and dense
and she forgot about everything else.

      This isn't a sad story because there are no sad stories

unless tellers want them; they control the telling, the withholding,
        the fortunate and unfortunate bend and stretch. Sometimes
        it's hard to find something more agile, as agile
        as a story

            nimbly sidestepping sadness

            because no story told goes all the way to the ending,
            the light's out of storytelling and fact-finding;

        the story of surviving it, survived
                the Permian mass extinction

      and stretched into us over thousands of years.

      The recognizably human comes out of it
            and the butter that the human recognizes

        whether in Timbuktu or Tokyo. There are connections, layovers:
        the power does not come here till after a pass through
        the substation and transformer. Deirdre takes me

to Tokyo Rose collection,

elixir of love body crème, body butter

       and on the same page:
       Be nice elf soap[13]

that scrolls
to Tanaka of Japan[14], menu pulled down, rolled up in spices

       —never mind: seems I read the *blush* of the search results
       as sweet blue wine

but this is verifiable:

Snow Brand Foods president Koshiro Iwase announced Friday
       the company's liquidation.[15]
On Saturday, parent Snow Brand Milk had its own apology to make.
On Saturday, Deirdre was dead.

       The company's managing director apologized to the public
       after the revelation that Snow Brand rewrote the expiration date by one year on
       760 tons of frozen butter.[16]

              —Milk scandal in 2000—

Snow Brand Milk is still trying to recover
from a tainted-milk scandal that left 14,500 customers sick
in and around Osaka.

Snow Brand found itself with an inventory backlog of butter
after the poisoned-milk incident. The company blamed that disaster on
a power failure that led to bacteria growing in the milk.

So in March 2001, the company gathered 2,300 tons of frozen butter
that was past its sell-by date from its Betsukai factory,
in eastern Hokkaido.

Snow Brand extended the sell-by date by one year,
after testing the butter and discovering it was safe to eat.

Deirdre and I usually played it safe too and just listened
to the percussion of excess traffic in her marriage, some
jams, and right-of-way violations, failure to signal
when changing lovers' lanes, as if she'd also married

every undercurrent, unpinning, every pulse; we waited
for butter to be brought to us by a waitress in a butterfly
of scalloped partial nurse hat. Perhaps now (we did this
more than once) a butter bowl is being emptied of butter patties size
of square quarters into tote bags, cuffs, up the sleeves of patrons

eager to slog butter to a destination that will involve sleep
at some point, restlessness, shine from butter contact. Greased

purses till we were twelve. Butter on our knees when out of Vaseline
and we had to shine in church.

Some sleepwalkers go the butter distance
every night that sleep is interrupted.

Fear of (peanut) butter sticking to the roof of the mouth
—*arachibutyrophobia*— keeping the somnambulant moving.

With so much motion, sometimes they are lucky,
                    and even when they aren't, sometimes find

> *lyllons: [The] Welsh faeries. They are very tiny, smaller*
> *than the Tylwyth Teg, with light skin and hair.*
> *Their garments are silken and usually white in color. They love to eat*
> *fairy butter, fungus growing on the roots of certain plants, and*
> *toadstools. They love cleanliness*
> *and have been known to reward those who keep their*
> *houses especially immaculate* [17]

But in the main event, butter, though on the way home,
gets sidetracked, swept away, kidnapped off the beaten path
with Little Red Riding Hood, so there is more magnitude
in what it means that that basket of goodies was blessed,
the butter meant to massage the granny feet,
oil of cloves as if the grandmother is to be the feast

                    —a wolf would not be this particular:
                    young women as sushi tables, melted butter
                    in navel, suprasternal notch, any hollow:

Don't go there, Red; Let butter be brought home except
when there is *butyrophobia* in any of the rooms:
the fear that sunny walls of kitchen will melt

though someone will just think spilled lemonade, overflow
of egg yolks mixed thinner in a blender. Liquid butter waifs.

(beams)

Each room is also butter shrine hosted
on a homepage: from there to all shared butter.
Karen Butter [18] is right at home with it, *Tokyo*'s right on
the résumé; she claims certain comfort openly, could
have married it, did not necessarily

as butter could have been birthright, probably paternal
the butter pat sinking into potatoes a kind of bloody eye

on conception—yellowish plasma for everyone
comes after extracting red blood cells.

The Butter touch everywhere Karen Butter's hands go. The Butter feel
if she's touched. Double butter if she touches butter and it presses back
with any force at all.

Butter orbit. Perhaps she's primed for an offering
from *Butter Books* that Deirdre would have loved:

> *Blur : the making of nothing*
> *authors: Elizabeth Diller and Richard Scofidio.* [19]

For substance you'll have to go to
                    Funk Butter Travel Page [20]
at least partially intact with permanent intentions.
                    It will contain pictures from my travels

through much blurred Tokyo winter, tomato sunsets rubbed
          on the lens, the value of persistence

                    put on whatever's shot

& willing to be seen in the light available; some always is, the context
          for blur's nonexistence which otherwise
          couldn't be mentioned, couldn't be ascertained.

In the abyssal level of the ocean, you bring your own
light from within

as if in the profundity, survival depends on having
eaten halos: the aura

of saints tends to be golden, a charmed buttery state

forced upon them by artists
for whom they can be as conventional as bread,
on which more is forced: transfiguration of the loaf, whole wheat:
       whole feast. The vow of poverty taken on by yeast,
       single cells in the budding Order Saccaromyces.

       Yeast priests. Saccharomycetes reproduce asexually,
       have lost all mycelium. Whole feat.

Our Lady's night is every night
she is thought of

for buttery intervention in heaven
               from which butter will drip medicine

       at Warszawa, With Miroque · Asian Gothic Presents Smooth Like Butter
       at On . . . 3opm · Dance Exhibition 2oo3 at New National Theatre Tokyo ·
       Toshi Ichiyanagi

       23 Wednesday Ladies Night at Fiddler, Half Price Cocktails & Wine ·
       Jimmy Angel at What the Dickens! · Robin Loochie Blues Duo/Trio at
       Bourbon Street in Roppongi, 9:3opm, Call o3-5786-2887 For Info ·
       Scramble Gig From SXDW 2oo3 at Club Asia, ¥25oo, 5:3opm, Invisible
       Man's Death Bed, Papaya Paranoia · Tumor Music Vol. 9 at Shelter,
       ¥2ooo, 7:3opm, The Strikers, Four The MG, Vasallo Crab 75 · Pea
       Planet Animation Festival 2oo3 at Cinema Rosa · AGUAGALA
       WORKSHOP at movement space GAMBETTA[21]

Because   If the opening intro of Tokyo Xtreme Racer Zero doesn't impress
             you with it's awe-inspiring sights and sounds, then
             nothing on television in this day and age will either.

Certainly not blur, the intro to closing Deirdre.

       Once into the game, the cars you race in and against
       are strikingly realistic . . . *Genki* spared no expense
       in making the cars   look like butter.[22]
The houses look like butter, too. The horses.

Butter speaks of kindred shaping. City festival, graduation,
reception:

your face sculpted in butter

or on black bread canvases
for digestive galleries.

These are cures in alternative medicine.
This is the way it should go. Butter residencies

in apothecaries.

In under an hour, a man with one leg,
the best way to single him out of the crowd doing this,
carved an entire butter army

and then there was a contest to defeat it, and it was defeated,
and an entire army was in one stomach. The carver had carved
no weapons for his army. Every soldier
was a general soldier, nondescript

—necessary for the time constraint, the detail an hour could hold.

They had no mouths.

Where he pushed in with fingernails, resulted at best in chins.

They had no mouths.

In the end, he went home successful
until daybreak
when the yellow flooded

so thoroughly even his spirit
was back in the butter

so he took a bath.

Because he commandeered so much for the army,
I suspect a shortage

of butter
and reasons:

> There is what happens
> and only what happens

when the story touches the tongue that tells it.

From the mouth, the story takes on the span of oil
meander on water surface, air spread, sound waves
in a ripple of unseen accordion-pressed peacock feathers,

> arrows actually

on target for ears.

Response is the problem, and
it is asked for, graded, rewarded, condemned

> —how terrible the ingenuity of response

to the story that cannot be blamed
for its moments of coincidence

and extraordinary accident
which is also the story of the world.

> Every story
can be told through a search for butter
if diligence prospers; I will find Deirdre again,

wasp waisted, human-chorionic-gonadotrophin free, in a B (is for Butter)
film where a string pulled the rest of the way, cuts through life

> —wire through cheese, eyelash through butter:
> I am impressed

with the extraordinary accident of the moment
when everything but the sky is blue:

Blue butter. Blue pages. Horrendous blue tongues
of nightingales.

In listening to horrendous tongues doused
with the entanglement of elementary orchestration,
her son just ten then,

Praise happens

for Joan Lock's Non-Fiction Books:[23]
Reluctant Nightingale
'forthright, funny and sad in turn' Women's Journal

Blue Murder?
'one you should not miss' Police Review

Every listing, every breakthrough and good idea
is a recycling of alphabet. Its infinite forms
wrap my tongue and brain in gods I cannot perceive
only pronounce; I am always mouthing something,
about to say to Deirdre:

spein ny hostyllyn	spiosal	spoag
apostle spoon	embalm, spice	buttercup
speyr-ghorrym	spittag	spoodragh
sky-blue, cerulean	sharp-tongued woman,	bad beer
	verbose woman, vixen,	spyrryd buigh
speyragh	shrew, spitfire	hydrochloric acid
frame aerial, climatic		
spiosaghey	spittag oie	S'taitnyssagh!
spice, embalm	nightingale	How charming![24]

Nothing lost, misplaced, adulterated, abridged in translation
of ashes to ashes, dust to dust, link to missing link:
I am whispering at her grave. I am walking on

Eggs.—[AUTHOR'S NOTE [[edited by this author]]:
The mockingbird lays beautiful eggs,
with much variation in color and markings.
The prevailing shape is ovate.
The ground varies from bluish white or greenish
white; "Nile blue" is a common shade.

Most of the eggs are heavily marked
with spots and blotches, more or less evenly distributed,
of various shades of brown, such as "hazel," "russet,"
"tawny," "cinnamon." One very odd egg before me is a spotless,
very pale blue, except for a dense solid cap at the larger
end of "cinnamon-rufous" overlaid with a ring of "hazel."]

[[Cook them in butter.]]
In this same position, where the mouse is,
Baird, Brewer, and Ridgway (1874) say:

"The vocal powers of the Mockingbird exceed,
both in their imitative notes and natural song,
those of any other species. Their voice is full,
strong and musical, and capable of an almost endless
variation in modulation. . . . In force and sweetness
the Mockingbird will often improve upon the original."

John Burroughs (1895) termed the mocker "Our nightingale"
and "Here is the lark and the nightingale in one."

It is that horrendous blue tongue, seen or not, documented or not
that gives the power to mock
beyond the design of the original.

The mockingbird's bluer flattery   that the mockingbird attacks

(frequently its own image in polished,
reflecting surfaces.[25])

Just as all should attack blasphemy.

⬆
⬇

[who are against it]

Blue-tongued blasphemy. Horrendous how
It licks blueness onto things. Licks it off.

Something is damaged by a blue coat
on; something is damaged with it off.

A night passes; on and off and on
until the bird faints, dies between.

It is not an isolated departure.

Blue flames wiggle gorgeously, famously
until closer, irresistible, they become gray
leavings.

World, blue planet, perhaps residue
of an accidental blow-out: all this from just one,
the bigness not large enough to blot out an accidental
possibility

                that makes me someone I shouldn't have to be,

the one for whom Florence Nightingale is anathema,
her bounteous results mocking what surfaces about Deirdre
in a search for Deirdre

—surely Florence Nightingale had her recipes, tinctures
after which her tongue was blue, was hours

robed in the color; its niece, so to speak,

the words tumbling in blue streams
so that it seemed her teeth pulled sometimes

on blue stretches of ill will, immoderate thoughts
that didn't make it into her Egyptian and Mediterranean journals,
        one bound in sumptuous blue cloth.

Surely she had a few unwholesome visions
that do not diminish her by an iota, visions much like these.

Blue blemish on her forehead, some
of the ink of what is her invention: *polar-area diagram
of the causes of mortality in the army in the east*

especially when consulting Nightingale, Florence.
*Notes on Matters Affecting the Health, Efficiency
and Hospital Administration of the British Army*, 1858[26].

She would not panic because of swelling and infection,
        the usual results of injury, especially as she was not hurt
        by this collision with praise

that prudence, once a common name, adjusted:

It has been said that Florence Nightingale was the first
to use diagrams for presenting statistical data. This is not true,
of course, but she may have been the first to use them
for persuading people of the need for change.[27]

As if answering that call for hygiene
in a nearby location,[28] she's a doll
—Blue tongue noticeably absent.
Few dolls have them, fewer demand them.

                              Some of the light of the lamp was blue

as if from cobalt
as if from Bengal light (deadly illuminating vapors
            that supported early photography, a love of peaceful pictures
            of Victorian death)

—as if portable pyrotechnics

            is in the hands of the angel of sepsis:

A flock of burns came
to kindling hands

and their smoke nested throughout the susceptible body,
clouds of bacteria and kindred electrons, unprecedented
enervating activity.

            There are blue trails: her footsteps, all too good,
            mostly unprecedented, but they may be walked in

on a *MN 109-HALF-DAY TOUR*[29]
to the Florence Nightingale museum & British Crimean cemetery

            Boat trip to the other side of Istanbul.
            Visit Selimiye barracks, which is the headquarters
            of 1.Army housing the museum of Florence Nightingale
            and then proceed to the British cemetery
            (Both places in military area, special permission
             required in advance).

St. Sophia, Blue Mosque, Ancient Hippodrome, Grand Bazaar.
On the Mosque: no external
visible space not covered with Arabic
that mapped movement of what circles minarets:
permanent records of snowflakes in transition,
signing a guest book, pilgrims who write *crystal*, *jubilee*,
and *revelation*. This is proof
that transience
is glorious. Florence

Nightingale is gone.   Snow
often articulates as feathery as implications
of her name: cells
of wings speaking of immortality and infinity,
melting in translation:

> *If you are possessed of discernment joined*
> *with knowledge, seek the company of the dervishes*
> *and become one with them,*[30]

the living snow.

The best historic attempts to photograph snowflakes
took place in Jericho, Vermont where

> *generally speaking, the western quadrants*
> *of widespread storms or blizzards*
> *furnish the most beautiful and perfect form*[31]

of snow

that sprang up on Bentley's doorstep before heading
to New Hampshire, then to Maine, Prince Edward Island;
shavings off crowns and majesty drop.

Denigration is a form of tribute;

from the same ultimate root, the house
of everything.
                When that house is just a mouth,
blue tongues make the mad speak madly.   Everything

said before becomes antecedent to the most terrible butter of all:
peak butter, apex butter; from this butter, is descent.

It's hard not to think of some form of terrible belly.
It is sickening. Florence Nightingale got sick
and eventually died
                                    —but down there it is easier to

Think of the ways to turn a tongue blue, to keep it blue, to genetically
alter the course of evolution for a harvest of much more chromatic skin
without oxygen deprivation—cyanosis: the beautified form of lack;

Think of tattooing blue tongues
all over the body;

Think of methylene blue drinks and their sponsorship
of blue pee.

Think of how blue teeth interact with butter, how after the bite
there is superficial look of rotten blue cheese, and no significant
forfeiture of any blueness of enhanced enamel.

Think of as many ways as you can to do justice to a nightingale:
some of them will be blue:
> Harpocration relates that the eyes and heart of nightingales, laid about men
> in bed, keep them awake. To make one die for sleep, dissolve the eyes and heart
> and give them secretly to the victim
> to drink; he will never sleep, but will so die,
> and it admits not of cure.

> Andrew Crosse, an English country gentleman,
> in 1837 made the following experiment, which excited much publicity:
> he mixed two ounces of powdered flint with six ounces
> carbonate of potassa, fused them with heat, reduced the compound
> to powder and dissolved it in boiling water, obtaining
> silicate of potassa. This he diluted in boiling water, slowly saturating
> with hydrochloric acid. This he then subjected to
> "a long-continued electric action, through the intervention
> of a porous stone" in an effort to form crystals of silica.
> This did not happen,
> but on the fourteenth day of the experiment, he observed
> a few minute whitish lumps on the middle of the electrified stone.

By the eighteenth day, these had grown and stuck out seven or eight filaments.
On the twenty-sixth day, they had become perfect insects,
standing erect on a few bristles, which were their tails.
On the twenty-eighth day they moved their legs, detached
themselves from the stone, and began to move about.
Perhaps a hundred insects were thus generated, pronounced
as belonging to the genus Acarus.
The insects were called Acarus Crossii[32]

and were called the favorite food
of blue-tongued nightingales, and the food
most loved by chickens

      and absolutely the only resolve when faced
with an inscrutable pregnant craving

—and all of them were so blue, obnoxiously so,
seeking that horrendous blue tongue

      that makes the butter bearable

      (for Deirdre most of all).

Let me tell you about a house on which the shingles
were its bangs. No neater bangs have ever been
anywhere. I mean no insult to Deirdre's bangs
which were limp petals gathered into barrettes.
Flat-eared shutters. Flirting windows only
when Venetian blinds winked scandal for an hour.

Some arrows of light are peacock feathers
which Deirdre could see were failed lightning.

It fell like brushes
with death too weak to spread butter.

      The wood of only its east wall was white
      and wasps repented and resided
      in the temple at the roof's inverted v-angle.

      Once, every neighborhood had a house like this,
      once there was also Naveen.

In a blue section of Florence, Alabama

it was a dream house
so wasn't meant to be built. Deirdre's mother's floor plan
had rooms that were really poorly conceived labyrinths,
even though there are no doors. She did not get a good grade
in home economics and used pale unsalted butter
in her sagging cakes flavored with anisette: the abstainers' rum.

> *In the paper of the wasp nest in the temple of the apex,*
> *there is as much history as there is anywhere else.*
> *The ashes of history become dust that is so fertile*
> *it grows more history. Dust is a mother.*

> Deirdre is dust.

> *One day the children were alone*
> *so briefly, it seemed time had not had time*
> *to pass.   Only three children*
> *but they could amplify their voices*
> *in arguments and laughter—one ever giving way*
> *to the other; one ever helping the other bore through wood,*
> *prodding wasps to dance away both envy and pity.*

> *They could not conceive of a dungeon*
> *though one was there, as dragons tend*
> *to have bellies of fire, even a quiet dragon*
> *of wooden legacy with wasps in the apex*
> *of its brain. Fire sleeps too.   Some say*
> *Prometheus wept then bathed in warm smoke*
> *of a roasting peacock roasting a nightingale*
> *that fell on the peacock's blue back.*

> *There is privilege of living in a form of dinosaur,*
> *tamed tails of walkway, a neighborhood*
> *of planked and shingled skin too pretty to be captivity.*

> *The mother had gone for provisions. Again*
> *she'd run out of what she needed, no matter*
> *how much she'd acquired.*

> Forty-nine years of Deirdre and now what?

Circumstances were normal.
So few depend on our permanent collections. Some of which
are recurring visions of anemones that mean nothing but ocean
and reef, and when they are gone, they still mean nothing
but they mean nothing better then.

There is a vastness in some Italian waters that means
emptiness. Deirdre could float like a manatee

and believed she'd get our

goats

when she walked on open air, that ocean, with

water skis,

and the rope that was a very long ripcord.   Our uncle
who doesn't know anyone anymore, barbecued a goat
for every holiday and funeral. He slaughtered them

first.

The barbecuing was their funeral
Our lack of blue food was absolute.

Before the mother of three can return
her arms filled with milk, butter, eggs, and a chicken

plucked clean as the sky above her, above the provisions,
the house, wasps, and children; before

she can put a key into one of the many locks
       —the keyhole a cutout of the dark head of a covered

woman—*the house catches fire, smoke begins moving*
like an enchanted blanket of suffocating evening, remnants
of a magic carpet that itself has been tricked:
       the huddle of children weighing it down

in the highest bedroom, in the apex
of their lives, milk and butter on the way, with their mother
in the glow

of a stoplight, signaling to make a left turn
onto the last few miles of asphalt atop a brick road.

A man in a T-shirt is on the roof trying to smash in
the bars still doing their job of keeping out intruders,

he is navigating a skid; he is trying to steer three children
that he is calling Shadrach, Meshach, *and* Abednego.

The mother has the radio on station WSMA
and looks in the rear view mirror that catches clouds
a white Bronco
in the form of hand, one gloved like an usher's.

On the roof: more people
with crowbars, tire irons, wrenches, and adrenaline.

The airbags deployed world-record muffins

Smoke-coaxed young throats swallow what blooms
right out of a surah
about arrivals of anguished angels like blue streaks

when men and women on the roof take small matters   into their hands
through the bars and squeeze out news over the wired service of touch:

with all that power, angels are hot, blue streak angels: the hottest:
flying generators, their motors are never turned off, they always run
hot
—and come to crown heads blue. Then silent prayer
acknowledges small things   by absorbing their whispers.

Soft smoke: The children's hair so

Bluish.

They pop out like Jiffy-pop Swami hats,
those airbags; they pop out chef hats.
I like the recipes on road signs:
rest, stop, yield, merge, exit;
with ten miles for construction,
there's time to put together something

from the apex of the warmth of young fingers
for the mother who's home now with butter, milk, eggs
and submersion of disappointment over nothing from peacocks
or nightingales into news; immediately she knows the man
speaking is not a prophet: *we held their hands*

until the end of lullabies. Bluish-brown residue:
of the mother of altars

on 6 July 2002[33]

The Eastern Stars file in
white shoulder to white shoulder

vulture's cape of dark hair on their necks, collars
darkening with visible lines of thunder

footwork assurance of rumble:
and they are Alps of Eastern Stars,
they are Adirondacks around Deirdre,
they are guardrails. After impact, I lean to look into

The Valley of Deirdre filling with mist:
      sparkling cobwebs
      limp harp strings
  placenta
    the day eats up
until bright's left.
There's nothing

but illumination.[34]

A Geologic Survey of Appetite

Rearrangements of food pleased him

the sound of utensils and crystal in action produced tension and tango in the kitchen

Teron did activate tectonic plates of sesame zucchini
and pumpkin butter autumn biscuits, pushing carrots into obelisks
and plums into mountain ranges that his teeth promptly eroded.
He felt full of vulture,

his shadow benign and graceful
as it moved in, shrinking shawl around a kill,
with a prowess of its own: toothless
black bottom flatiron smoother.
His own shadowed face had absolutely no concerns.

His tongue seemed to Reena who watched her son lick shadows clean
like a parboiled slug and also like something she should peel
then sauté in a skirt of bay leaves, after which it would be blistered
with poppy seeds, sequins that had lost their brilliance
to Reena whose new freckles glittered.

Beneath sequins: Velveeta cheese-blend glue.

She relished fresh guava relish.

—Reena, the evidence shows, had been seduced
by her own coriander.

How pretty were the eggs that Teron hadn't eaten, whites
collaring three yolks scooped out to hold cilantro
and chopped celery, chopped olives, fried onion crumbles & dust,
white pepper, slivers of cherimoya with burnt ends.
Pieces of prayer.
—it just cracked up!
Traces should be left cosmetic on the face.

Still there was incompletion
so Reena went into the yard to pick blue flowers
that wouldn't have been there if things hadn't moved
from what they once were in time.

Light led her to harebell and wild lupine,
blue roses who'd sucked the sky clear leaving crippled light;
blue roses whose stems she placed to pierce spice

that reached out from under a sheet
of nut-oil laminated egg white. It lacked muscle
yet gripped a place setting Reena liked, stepping away,
looking back. In an hour

Original purpose was cold, lost
unlike original sin. Reheating rubberized the egg:
Cosmic looking hubcap.

She became aware of

        The life cycle of motors.

Octane-rated vigor blood and death blood (twin engines)
spilled in a swimmable pool (microorganisms present)
at the scene of a murder
                (chlorine the weapon of mass micro-destruction)

and rust as ravaging heartache and arthritis of machines:
Grizzly times.

The taste of life in dead meat
                     is what she wanted.
    Some rev.

But it was pure Morphometry. In service to the outside. Everlasting
strip and peel: any surface revealed by delving is the outside
of something also a gate and trapdoor to the deeper.

Skeletons placed directly into the earth without coffins
coming up like a crop of sculpture.
Armadillos in the houses of Human Patellae.
Pachyderm patellae evicting human skulls.

Bone sprout.
Aspiration takes longer to die than the body.

The art of infestation didn't bother Teron: definitely Reena's son:
flies and worms unknitting flesh tailoring how he'd put things
together. Carrion animals gathering around indisposed mothers
and fathers whose bodies still performed parental duties:
feeding the young
without species bias, just as the human parents themselves
had freely partaken of cow and sheep's milk; later: also
the leather.

Putrefaction was interesting to Teron, reassuring:
the point was to simplify, reduce; soup's on.

How extraordinary: All the possible human odors
and how task-specific odors are:

In the religion of rituals of decomposition
the body didn't have to say a word, just emit odors,
results.

His parents had taken him to a number of open-casket funerals
of strangers so that Teron could see corpses. They thought that better
than arranging a tour of morgues. He was funeral home schooled.

~ *The Viewing of Edna Alston* ~

Though she is so leathery that in her casket
she seems a suitcase inside a suitcase,

Teron looks for signs that dreams still occur
although Edna had her brains blown out by a boyfriend.
How well her skull has been restored, how the family insisted,
not on a wig, but on actually transplanting hair into her
revamped scalp.
For Edna,
the family purchased hair from women they trusted
were recently deceased nuns
who'd at least once visited the Vatican and bathed
in blessed water. They seem so certain
of what's on Edna's head.
Maybe it's really from some sleek animal
blessed to be mink or otter.

They believe the hair on Edna.

Given access to the miniscule, given the life on worlds
in the deep space of electron microscopes, whole zoos
on a single slide; universes of what lives in Edna's new hair
will be buried alive.

The Continent of Reena and Marcus' Marriage

Marcus was most fond of coriander
for cutting a trench into his tongue

and hiding there to pond his coffee
and trap the smell of the sour pillow rolls
(as if flavored with baby sputum)
Reena made which should be famous:

a mix of rye and corn meal, safflower oil, aging
(come-back baby) milk, and shredded pumpkin to be silk,
dill, pine nuts and seeds his teeth cracked;
rolls indented in the center that Reena promised—by the way
she buttered only the hot depression—was a scale model
of the indentation of her head on his shoulder on his pillow.
(Once.)

While pregnant, she made ginger soy and honey pepper rolls
that, once filled with toasted sugared mums, became oddly
luminescent,
and he had prospered
from watching Reena swallow crumbling bites, fireflies
sparkling through the delicate skin of her neck
as they went all the way down. Commonwealth

of disintegration.

He wondered whether or not the light should get wet,
unable to conceive, for the moment,
of any kind of bioluminescence, just electrical sources
and surges, inner lamp, the umbilical cord an electrical cord

plugged into the back of Reena's navel, pig snout an alternate
standby socket in a self-frying generator if necessary

and he feared it would be, & out of overloaded love feared that immersion
in water while Reena was so electrified might kill her

      (The fire-breathing dragon breathes fire outwardly: it is fire
      of exhalation, but this was fire of total respiration: breathed out and in,
scorching, flaming interior bouquets of organs and shrubs
      of nerves)

      (The Blue Reena:
      perennial)

(the Blue Reena out of nowhere:

                  on the fourth of July: she blossoms further into
                  the Screaming Meanie)

      (hogs opportunity)

and just whips up out of the most inviolate Antarctic
or dervish winds, snowy cream and sugar dahlias,
some the size of flying saucers.

When Jennifer Shows Me a Wave in Form of Question[35]

I see the standard Aunt Lottie:
death no deviation

from her formaldehyde-fixed flip
of curl above her forehead:

model of park shelter, part of the slope
where Aunt Lottie conceived, stiff, paralyzed
with inexperience

still part of Aunt Lottie's careless reaching
as if to pluck her brows, snitch out betrayers
knitting an acrostic on her face
while she works with cadavers, breaking

the neck to better style hair fixed so much
with spray: Aunt Lottie's really into fumigation:

the sepsis if any's in her eyes
(—for looking at what she looks at
instead of the faces she kisses,

locations where brains used to be,
her fist in rib cages that open like any others—)

is ruined (evicted) by the formaldehyde
her latexed fingers put there, her eyes floating
in it: knockoff artificial tears in her receptacle head
one day on a similar slab of table

for family approval
of how natural it was for her to be in a morgue:
hit music on, rhythmic reflex pop-up
of buoyant corpses full of gas and fluid, slurping
of carbonated beverages as thick with ice
as Lottie's eyes are dense with preservation.

It was after the embalming that she was frozen,
sent to a glacier per last request
instead of a cryogenic chamber
whose liquid nitrogen if frozen makes too many

patterns of ghost mistletoe. Hers will be compromised
revival at best. Under a curl of ice:
solidity, as usual: only a matter of temperature,
that magnifies her cursive c-curl bangs:
Aunt Lottie's staged
for an avalanche to dive, take her in
when no ground will. A scooping up of her

by a cold, cold curled shovel

as heartless as the last man she worked on:

his marrow in a child with bones like birds,
his corneas on hold, half his tongue
a testicular pouch for post-cancer sensitivity,
his speechless stub restored
as diving board and runway with the swatch
of red carpet Aunt Lottie tacked on the wood
where kisses made his taste buds blossom
into reefs of pansies in the flood, tidal wave, tsunami
of passion drowning him up to his head

bald as Aunt Lottie's ice floe.

The Culture of Reena and the Bear

Before the Bear: derived from a theory of gravy

(The neckline and hem of Reena's gown
were trimmed with real hummingbirds
[just a few tiny pins in the outspread wings
—she could feel the racing unison
that the tiny hearts fell into] and actual orchids.
The beak closest to it tried to extract nectar
from the small cleft—the suprasternal notch—
at the bottom of her perfumed throat)

(Bees drew near; live jewels from the garden.)

Breakfast Before the Bear: ocular effects

She still had her eyes and others too
on a tray: unpitted olives
coated with a thin layer of meringue
as vitreous humor substitute
that she placed in each bowl of owlet soup
in which floated owl embryos braised
in butter and chives, sprinkled with brandy
just before serving, and skewered
with knife-length pieces of jicama,
tasting slightly of rodents
the parent owl had eaten, ambiance
of background radiation, a theorem of alternatives,
the microworld of taste, from here
the same as a comet's rat's tail
coming from between her teeth,
a glittering skeleton, tendon flex
of her reaction attaching Reena
to the muscle of how hard the universe works.

Before the Bear: Reena's first marriage

preceded by romance.
They exchanged rings
like the bands on goose legs.

     Promise her anything: give her foie gras:
     stuff it down her throat

The Culture of Reena and the Bear

Once she began wondering what it would be like to eat her way
out of something, she did something about it: came to bed
in an open-fire roasted clove-studded carcass of beef
(the cloves are the dried unopened flower buds of a tree
called the Zanzibar Red Head).

Unfortunately, the bear though as hungry as it should be
after hibernation respected the presence of Reena's husband,
so with him there the bear alone wasn't illuminated;
Reena couldn't hold on to just its light
and lost sight of its darkness in the darkening evening's
Bear hug.

The Superior Love of the Macurap in the Amazon without Reena
Who's Busy Looking at Ursa Major and Minor

For their efforts the Macurap of the Amazon have
viscous jelly destiny of the broth
maintained for a week as one by one
Macurap women kill their husbands: the intensity of their love
finally at a boiling point: the body everywhere: inside
and out, sensitive to what touches, digesting
intestinal love, cud climax, deep marriage
in the pit of heavenly bellies even more transformation:
husbands taken to limits of what can be taken
in: husbands becoming ultimate alphabet of pleasure: extracts
of A, B, E, vitamin K, crystalline pyridoxine: vitamin B_6,

vitamin P: bioflavonoid from rinds and husks:
Macurap wives watch their husbands eat some.
Citrus whispers roasted into his lungs,
tincture of balsam, fermented boil, white peppered
with grubs and lice, lips smack on
how nothing else tastes like a man
loved to death. His cleaned rib cage
is a bone cape around her; her legs twine
around his femurs
as she makes love to ivory scepters.

Reena & the Three Bears

Golden locks on the pleasure cupboards
can be polished or opened;

grand openings

so much more tasteful
than the proprietor down the road
who called that first of several popular
while-you-wait tailoring shops
Jack the Ripper.

Meet Reena the Butcher.
Fresh bear meat for this girl hunter.

The braided rug's circumference is enlarged
by blood-spray

into an alien dahlia of blood
that is just right.

Mulberry Breath as Proof of the Wave in Form of Question[36]

Jennifer, here are some facts bred by the others:

a polar bear's fur is not white.
Each hair shaft is pigment-free and transparent
with a hollow core

that scatters and reflects visible light,
much like ice, snow, and other cold partnerships

When photographed with ultraviolet sensitivity,
polar bears appear black.

Because they give off no detectable heat,
they do not show up in infrared capture.

A scientist's infrared snapshot,
produced a single spot: the puff of air

caused by the animal's breath

so trust it. It will not lie. If it has toxins
it will give them to you.   That which is airborne
overcame drag and coefficients. Air will let
almost anything pass through it —why do you think

souls always get away?   The fact that basic air
doesn't make itself conspicuous is in its favor:
                                    —most of it is nitrogen
that seldom gets attention which goes to minority oxygen
but they don't bother with trading places: I fear air

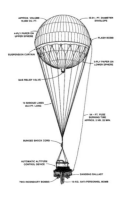

is polluted with perfection: kites, balloons; breathers
can see the gas come out: balls of our electricity float:
that's what's in us   —but there is transience

among balloons expanding into a battalion
of odd lollipops, in that same family of don't-take-candy-
from-strangers unless it's Halloween:
some balloon sophisticates
that came to Oregon, Seattle, Wyoming,
one to the open outskirts of Detroit from Japan

released in the winter jet stream
to burn when they landed   what they touched:
initially the spirit,

the actual descent like that of gift
of alien interpretations of angels
as nonhuman as our versions

      (the immortality for one
      and sufficient, usual thing):

              mulberry paper balloons,[37] potato flour, expansive hydrogen
                         in November, arrival in
                         Thermopolis, Nogales,

                              and Bly
                  where a minister, his wife, five
                    Sunday school pupils
          experienced fisherman's luck, catching
          the balloon, pulling it through the trees
               as they would their savior
            in form of cross that fifth of March

      preoccupation with Easter on top of war

      —through even cheap binoculars:
      a patch of mulberry paper became the whole sky:
      a scrap on the lens.

I also didn't see (till now)
how much like, turned on its side,

a chart of the eye this gift is: focal point,
the so-put-upon retina,
images falling short, going too far
requiring other names for vision:
myopia, hyperopia, utopia

with cockeyes, convergent strabismus, cross-eye:
garnishes, painting, the day's featured menu

peered at with bifocals
for a chance at recognizing everything.

La cultura de pescada:
a prediction (instead of promise)
 —for Larry

Light is desperate—*Licht ist hoffnungslos* so
just before we finish arriving at the limit of the theoretically possible
universe in la cultura de pescada, *de cultuur van vissen*
the sensible horizon passes through the eye of the spectator
at right angles to the vertical at this place given to us
ripe with, like all places: the residue of orchids.
Even in that much—residue of that magnitude—even
residue translates as longing
therefore often also as betrayal, mild at times

such as *when the plane is parallel to the sensible horizon of a place*
so that *it passes through the earth's center and becomes celestial*
horizon: somehow—believe me—

we arrive at the beginnings of the theoretically improbable:
die Anfänge vom theoretisch unwahrscheinlichen:
our own defied impossibility. As soon as possible
we will have:
a belly-open fish as waterproof hat,
the gift of heavy gar hair
demanding back-breaking work as the gars' maid, their chauffeur,
the body a vehicle for so much implication, indictment
because there's no prediction that can't be fulfilled
with forms of bankruptcy:
the fish heads milked, gobbled in air reluctant to intervene, calm
atmosphere, composed as the moon's dead sea of tranquility, fossilized
panic, transistor radios unearthed for their good parts:
amplifiers & rectifiers,
replacement nipples,
elbows, knees (the bendables, the crooks)
that look as if they should contain coconut milk

that comes from a hairy beast (really as if sliced off the chest
of a particularly buxom, more human ape) of a fruit of a fish among
a sea of palms kelping in the current of air, opening and closing
like hula hands more the color of muddy rivers than of paradise:
good trout hands, brown crappie hands, touch of eczema
breaks through mehendi, rough magic: *one fish, two fish, red fish, blue fish*:

the doctor's call, powdery pests
also on palm fronds blackening at edges: permanent
as from repeated applications of kohl: lids and eyes
dark as mines, explosive, the neem fish huddled in limb schools:
none so dense that sky can't be seen through them—look up:

between fronds: blue prom necklaces:
bony places

reduced to
sliver

of light through them, then totality of eclipse
sustained: dark's eye's slow infinite wink

at me, celestial as a fish made of stars

plus the wow of astronomical diamond ring (in a moon pass,
round dead ship)
fitted to the hand held up, covering completely
the jelly-jar lid apparent
size of the star of black-out:

It's in my hand

:

visiting a place where there's cholera, hours of radio
silence, where someone has brought their own malaria,
has partaken of local typhus,
where I ride double-decker busses
on which every passenger has a telescope
pulled out when the bus attacks winding ascending roads
—looking as if the lot of us empties a beer bottle
into our eyes

—looking as if the lot of us pull dull black swordlets
from our eyes

—looking as if the lot of us are fishing:
none of the individual stars magnified by this,
but the number of stars is

and also the cosmos of insects
that the double-decker's windshield accumulates:

as many insects in the sea of air
as stars in the sea of infinity
as fish in the culture of fish:

la cultura de pescado / die Kultur der Fische / la culture des poissons
la coltura dei pesci / a cultura dos peixes / de cultuur van vissen

the culture of gar

la coltura del luccio
   die Kultur des Kaimanfischs   *de cultuur van geep*
     la culture de l'orphie

    la cultura del gar

      —dei orchids —dos orchids

die Kultur der Orchideen

—de orquídeas

culture of orchids
derivatives and hybrids

:

✓ the climate of fish adhering beautifully
 to the orchids of skin

  ✓ *el clima de pescados que adhieren excepcionalmente a las orquídeas de piel*
  ✓ *il clima dei pesci che si aderiscono nel silenzio perfetto ai orchids di pelle*
  ✓ *o clima dos peixes que aderem belamente aos orchids da pele*
  ✓ *das Klima der Fische, die schön an den Orchideen der Haut haften*
  ✓ *le climat des poissons adhérant comme la peau aux orchids de la peau*

beautifully
the orchids of skin
loosen: la cultura at my feet,
toenails, gar scales

sense of completion: *Richtung der Beendigung*
clima perfecta

point of connection: towering orchids, culture of clouds, skin
like the day's catch of fishes at the Kyobashi Bridge

Richtung der Beendigung   ::   this is horizon

> *Aufsätze der Orchideen, Kultur der Wolken, Haut an der Kyobashi Brücke*
> *tours des orchids, culture des nuages, peau au pont de Kyobashi*
> *torrette dei orchids, coltura delle nubi, pelle al ponticello di Kyobashi*
> *torres dos orchids, cultura das nuvens, pele na ponte de Kyobashi*
> *torres de las orquídeas, cultura de nubes, piel en el puente de Kyobashi*

communion: culture of clouds, towering orchids,
                                        falling
skin like, black like rain of fishes: endless yesterday in Kigali

> *negro como la lluvia de pescados*
> *preto como a chuva dos peixes*
> *nero comme pioggia dei pesci*
> *schwärzen Sie wie der Regen der Fische*
> *noir comme la pluie des poissons*

Black glue / memory goo: we go to in Kigali at both ends of Kyobashi:

> *pegamento negro, goo de la memoria;*
> *colagem preta, colla near, schwarzer Kleber,*
> *Gedächtnis goo; colle noire, goo de mémoire:* the back absorbs

the weight of gar:[38]
                              les poids de l'orphie,
      das Gewicht—il peso—des Kaimanfischs—del luccio; they disappear:
                        —verschwinden—sparisce
into the nidus-hump of dorsal pregnancy:
dorsale Schwangerschaft, birth
of towers of powers of memory: do not forget:
Like impossible birds: heaviness flying:
the earth and its obligations and purgatories (including multitudes
of penguins negotiating cliffs and rocky towers in bare webbed feet) winged:

Everything is like that: *tutto è come quello, todo es como ése*

towering, hanging

> *—frutas en los arboles como pescado,*
> *las hojas como pescado, cada folha como peixes, ogni foglio come pesci,*
> *ogni frutta——jedes Blatt ist ein Fisch; jedes Frucht*
> *——chaque feuille est poisson——elk fruit, elk blad is een vis;*

>> every fruit, every leaf a fish

>> all space is a sea of something: todo
>> espacio es mar: mar: mar

>> if there's nothing: ¡es una mar de nada

>> magnifica!   ¡Mira!:

les pinecones sont crabes, langoustines——
die pinecones sind Krabben, Hummer——
i pinecones sono granchi, aragoste——

>> the pinecones are crabs, lobsters

——os pinecones são caranguejos, lagostas——zeekreeften
  ——los pinecones son cangrejos, langostas——

on breezes: *brisas, gefluister, brezze, Brisen,*
whispers: *chuchotements, Flüstern, bisbigli, sussurros:*

the longing—(for the sea of the theoretically improbable:
die Anfänge vom theoretisch unwahrscheinlichen: our own defied
impossibility) —the longing—

> *para ellos, per loro, para eles, pour eux, für sie—*
> *het longing voor hen:*

for them.[39]

Refined Search (highly selective)

appetite: vii, 108, 127

flower: vii, 18, 23, 28, 33, 39, 48, 49, 54, 56, 63, 65, 66, 72, 73, 74, 75, 76, 79, 80, 83, 84, 108, 111, 116, 12, (sun*flower* : 19, 52, 84)

—dahlia: 75, 112, 117, 127

—peony: 56, 80, 127

—pollen: 39, 48, 63, 64, 71, 73, 127

—blossom: 54, 65, 70, 74, 83, 84, 88, 112, 114, 127

—stem: 20, 49, 54, 66, 73, 109, 127

—system: iv, 13, 54, 82, 83, 87, 127

—leaf: 125, 127

—leave: 12, 38, 40, 44, 66, 72, 81, 84, 88, 108, 127

—cleave: 80, 127

—cyclamen: 65, 75, 127

—phlox: 80. 127

—nerium: 80, 127

—pistil: 56, 79, 127

—buttercup: 80, 97, 127

radioactive: 74, 127 (*radio*: 11, 106, 121, 122)

atomize: 20, 127 (*atom*: ix, 11, 28, 33, 53, 57, 69; *atom*ic/sub*atom*ic: 53, 74)

glass: vii, 7, 9, 10, 11, 17, 18, 19, 46, 63, 86, 127

jar: 22, 89, 122, 127

dish: 39, 64, 127 (*dish*pan: 36)

radish: 66, 83, 127

crystal: 17, 68, 70, 81, 88, 101, 102, 108, 127 (*crystal*line: 65, 116)

transparent: 17, 79, 118, 127 (semi*transparent*: 17)

apparent: 122, 127

pig: 35, 59, 72, 78, 112, 127

—pigment: 118, 127

morphometry: 109, 127

coefficient: 118, 127

lens: 10, 93, 119, 127

orchid: 115, 121, 123, 124, 127 (*Orchid*een: 123, 124)

l'orphie: 123, 124, 127

clear: 8 (*clearly*), 17, 60, 65, 79, 85, 109, 127 (nu*clear*: 33, 35)

clarity: 10, 11, 68, 127

blur: 9, 10, 11, 20, 81, 93, 94, 127

—blurt: 66, 127

gefluister: 125, 127

gleam: 14, 16, 127

williwaw: 57, 127

phosphorous: 12, 16, 128

ambition: 128

ripple: 4, 75, 96, 128

—cripple: 13, 109, 128

tangle: 72, 83, 128

—entangle(ment): 31, 32, 34, 97, 128

—rectangle: 5, 128

fold: 4, 9, 22, 46, 58, 77, 88, 89, 128

—unfold: 46, 49, 89, 128

believe(r): 5, 22, 23, 32, 41, 90, 105, 111, 121, 128

—recommend: 88, 128

zygote: 68, 128

Columbo: 17, 128

anesthesia: 128

Endnotes

[1] Italicized lines and phrases are taken from, the lion's share: "Saint Francis and the Sow" by Galway Kinnell, and the rest from *Hidden Beauty* by France Bourély. This poem completes my efforts, publicly revealed in the essay "Contemplating the Theft of the Sow" (first published in Countermeasures: A Magazine of Poetry and Ideas7, presently viewable online at http://www.english.uiuc.edu/maps/poets/m_r/moss/essays.htm) to steal the sow.

[2] Surah 59:24

[3] Italicized lines and phrases are taken from, the lion's share: "Saint Francis and the Sow" by Galway Kinnell, and the rest from *Hidden Beauty* by France Bourély.

[4] John Whitfield in *Nature*, 19 June 2003

[5] John Whitfield quoting David Page in *Nature*, 19 June 2003

[6] some praise and gratefulness for my Interferon.

[7] takes off from Sam Abell's photographic account of a Mr. Wonderful in *Seeing Gardens.*

[8] http://www.winrock.org/what/volunteer/assignment.cfm?AC=GUI060

[9] http://www.schiercompany.com/ButterEquipment.html]

[10] http://www.ibiblio.org/herbmed/faqs/culi-4-5-butter.html

[11] http://www.itdg.org/html/itdg_southernafrica/small_enterprises.htm

[12] http://www.ncagr.com/fooddrug/fdrprog.htm

[13] hamptonct.com/index.cgi/cart_id

[14] tanakaoftokyohawaii.com/menu

[15] cnn.com/2002/BUSINESS/asia/02/ 25/japan.snowbrand.biz/?

[16] Alex Frew McMillan CNN Hong Kong

[17] http://laydylynx.tripod.com/etoj.html

[18] www.library.ucsf.edu/staff/butter

[19] www.butterpaper.com/resource/architects_overseas_01.htm

[20] www.funk-butter.com/index.html, http://www.funk-butter.com/Travels/index.htm, www.funk-butter.com/Travels/TokyoWinter01/bysea2.htm

[21] http://www.japan-zine.com/CalendarTokyo.htm

[22] http://www.psillustrated.com/teamps2/rz_tokyozero.html

[23] http://www.twbooks.co.uk/authors/joanlock.html

[24] http://www.ceantar.org/Dicts/Manx/mx44.html

[25] http://home.bluemarble.net/~pqn/ch31-40/mockingb.html

[26] (at http://www.agnesscott.edu/lriddle/women/nightpiechart.htm)

[27] http://www.york.ac.uk/depts/maths/histstat/small.htm

[28] http://www.dolls-viamaureen.com/f.florence2.html

[29] http://www.angelfire.com/vt/minostravel/mn109.html

[30] Farid al-din 'Attar; *The Speech of Birds*, translated by Peter Avery, published by the Islamic Texts Society f London, 1998.

[31] from the Introduction of the article "Photographing Snowflakes" by Wilson A. Bentley, born in 1865, the year a war finished its birth, really started its life in both blue and gray. The article was originally published in *Popular Mechanics* in 1922 and is offered currently as a Dover edition, in the Dover Pictorial Archive Series, 2000.

[32] http://www.iras.ucalgary.ca/~volk/sylvia/TheBestiaryProject.htm

[33] also the legal anniversary of my marriage in the dining room; the church wedding when I was beautiful almost two months later doesn't count, but is sacred

[34] Surah 53, *Al Najm* (The Star)

[35] for Jennifer Metsker who showed me the picture

[36] for Jennifer Metsker who showed me the picture again

[37] diagram from http://www.polarbearsalive.org/facts3.php#anchor766763

[38] Deirdre = the weight of Gar

[39] Italicized definitions are from *Webster's Revised Unabridged Dictionary*

Acknowledgments

Thanks to the editors of the following journals, in which the poems listed first appeared, sometimes in an earlier form:

American Scholar: "Mulberry Breath as Proof of the Wave in Form of Question"
Bat City Review: "The Culture of Glass"
Boston Review: "Victim of the Culture of Facelessness"
Born: "Jennifer Shows Me a Wave in Form of Question"
Callaloo: "The Culture of City Peaches," "The Small World Studies Pictures of Cadavers"
Columbia: A Journal of Literature and Art: "Ghee Glee," "The Culture of Mr. Wonderful," "The Culture of Reena and the Bear"
Cream City Review: "The Culture of Snowmen"
Gargoyle: "Heads wrapped in Flowers"
Konundrum: "The Unbuttered Subculture of Cindy Birdsong"
Michigan Quarterly Review: "La cultura de pescada: a prediction"
Poetry: "The Subculture of the Wrongfully Accused," "The Continent of Reena and Marcus' Marriage"

"Lake Deirdre" appeared in the anthology *Big Water*, edited by Alison Swan.

And thank you, Gabe, for enabling the shaping of *Tokyo Butter* that allows the lake to move as it should. Interactions are everything.

The diagram of the Japanese bomber balloon on page 119 is used by permission of the Smithsonian National Air and Space Musuem.

About the Author

Thylias Moss is the author of seven previous volumes of poetry, most recently *Slave Moth: A Narrative in Verse*, named Best Poetry Book of 2004 by *Black Issues Book Review*; *Last Chance for the Tarzan Holler*, a National Book Critics Circle Award finalist; *Small Congregations: New and Selected Poems*; and *Rainbow Remnants in Rock Bottom Ghetto Sky*, winner of the 1991 National Poetry Series Open Competition and the Ohioana Book Award. Her other books include a memoir, *Tale of a Sky-blue Dress*, and a children's book, *I Want to Be*. A 1996 Fellow of the MacArthur Foundation and a recipient of a Whiting Writer's Award, she has also received grants from, among others, the Guggenheim Foundation, the National Endowment for the Arts, and the Kenan Charitable Trust. She is a professor of poetics and creative writing at the University of Michigan, and lives in Ann Arbor.

Moss wrote *Tokyo Butter* employing an ideology she has termed Limited Fork Poetics, which she describes as follows:

> Limited Fork Poetics (LFP) believes that Poetry is a complex adaptive system, and because of that, page is unrestricted, and means "location of the poem." Some poems will inhabit places for which there is not yet means of detection or interpretation. A dynamic poem is event, occurs in time, and in its totality includes all versions, all drafts, all dread ends, all revisions, all versions, all thought that the person encountering a form of the poem supplies— this can be a reader (who remakes the poem through interacting with it) or what is considered the primary maker (poet) of the poem. A dynamic poem is a system of poetry, so (shifting) interactions between the subsystems (all that the poem contains) is essential to making (mutable) meanings. A dynamic poem hosts interacting language systems (including sonic, aural, and visual forms besides/in addition to/instead of text). The activity of interacting systems takes place on all scales simultaneously. The landscape of a single poem can include multiple areas of constituents of the poem taking shape in multiple forms (including sonic, aural, and visual forms besides/in addition to/instead of text) simultaneously, in varying degrees of stability (forms of accessibility/coherence) and instability (forms of inaccessibility/incoherence). There is no definitive beginning or ending. A portion (or portions) of a poem is joined, is left in progress. Interactions at a given time help determine the observable stability or instability (and the per-

ceived direction[s] of the activity). Metaphor is a tool of navigation that can enable instantaneous access to other event locations on any scale—akin to navigating worm-holes. The journeys to and from what is considered the same metaphorical events may not be identical.

There are many more possibilities for even the paper page than I could imagine before giving birth to LFP. Right now I like very much the implications of event horizon within LFP.